Empower Yourself Through Your Memories

Use the Lessons from Your Past to Create A Happy Present and Future

Printed in the United States of America

To all my past coaches, teachers, friends, family, and everyone who ever provided encouragement to me. Thank you for all the ways you helped me empower myself.

Contents

A Word about QR Codes

Throughout the book, at the beginning of each chapter, you'll find what is called a "Quick Response (QR) Code." Basically, it's a fancy phrase for a bar code. A QR code looks like this:

Simply scan the image with the camera on your mobile device and within seconds, you'll be taken directly to a video about the chapter. Go ahead, try it!

If you don't already have a QR reader on your device, you'll want to acquire one. These can be found in your app store. Many of them are free of charge.

If you don't want to use the QR reader, I've also provided a URL address that will take you to the same information. Here is the URL for this video:

http://www.phenomenalmemory.com/BookResources/video1.htm

Preface

After my first two books in the "Heal Your Memories" series achieved bestseller status. I wondered if there was anything additional that I could help people with the subject of healing your memories. "Heal Your Memories, Change Your Life" taught the reader to release the feelings from unhappy memories. "The Ultimate Guide To Healing Your Past" taught you that you can learn from any memory. Even if the memory happened years ago, you can still learn from it now.

Businesses have used the slogan "Empower yourself" since the early 1990's, and everyone wants to feel that they have some power and control in their lives. You could look at self-help and healing as a coin. On the tales side, you have to let go of the negative feelings and programming. The heads side is filling you with more positive thoughts and feelings.

In my "Heal Your Memories" series, "Heal Your Memories, Change Your Life" is the tales side. Learning from your memories from "The Ultimate Guide To Healing Your Past" is part of the heads side. However, in this book, I add empowering yourself to the heads side.

When you learn from your memories, you also need to apply what you have learned. "Empower Yourself Through Your Memories" will help you do it. It has the same format as the other books. You will read inspiring stories from people who empowered themselves through their memories and do exercises to empower yourself. However, if you have not read the first two books you do not have to read them to read this.

There are many ways that you can feel dis-empowered. You can feel shy is social situations, you could always be a follower and let the other person take the lead. Maybe you feel that you have no control over food and overeat. Perhaps you feel totally controlled at work and nothing you do is appreciated, so you will never advance.

These are just a few of the ways you can feel dis-empowered. Get set for an inspiring journey of self-empowerment.

Introduction

We all have memories. They are the mental records of our past. They come to us as thoughts, feelings, mental images, and personal scripts--those snippets of self-talk about the things we have experienced that make us who we are. Our memories hide in the recesses of our minds and come to the surface to remind us of our successes and failures, our strengths and weaknesses, and our fears and moments of intrepid fearlessness.

The difference between you, me, and Frank Healy is that, while we can recall our memories with some degree of detail, he, because of his photographic memory, remembers every memory in his life with crystal clarity. Because of this, his memories have the power to heal instead of just remember.

Once again Frank has used his own memory, experience, and the stories of amazing people to teach us how we can use our past to empower ourselves. His new book shows how everyone, not just those with amazing recall like himself, can use their memories to empower themselves and live the lives they want and deserve.

Dr. Richard Blonna

Chapter 1 QR Code

http://www.phenomenalmemory.com/BookResources/video2.htm

Chapter 1

Four Steps Toward Self-Empowerment

For the last fifty years of his life, he knew the date of everything that happened to him. He could recite any day of the week and tell you what the weather was like, what the news stories were on television, and what happened moment by moment in his life. His world became a tapestry of dates and events that he would never forget, even if he tried.

Pleasant memories and experiences are great to recall and meditate on. He discovered that he was never bored because, during any dull or uneventful moments, he could sift through all the things he remembered in his life and smile at the memories of family vacations, fun with friends, work accomplishments, and other good times. There were so many great things in his life that he remembered.

Not all of his memories would put a smile on his face though. Some were painful. He had memories of social rejection, bad days at school, and of course the unpleasant illness from time to time.

During his college years, he decided to study psychology and eventually learned techniques to let go of the painful memories. There were so many. For all those years, because of his ability to remember so many things, all the pain of those unpleasant experiences felt like a weight, not only on his shoulders but on his entire body and being. Learning to let go was liberating, to say the least.

Through his studies, he learned to categorize his memories into three imaginary filing cabinets. First, there was the shiny red cabinet where he kept all of his good memories and experiences. Next, there was a dark blue cabinet where he filed all of his painful memories. Although he could never forget the memories and the experiences held in this cabinet, he did learn to let go of the pain that was stored with them. Lastly, there was a gray cabinet which contained what he called mixed memories. These were experiences that were both good and bad, like the day in school when he got a good grade on a test and had fun with friends but then someone in one of his classes started trouble. Then there was the time he swam in the ocean with his grandchildren and had a ton of fun but then wound up with a bloody nose. Interestingly, this cabinet contained more memories than the first two. He learned that most of his days were a mixed bag. This seems true for most people.

After categorizing his memories and learning to let go of the pain from any unpleasant memories, he then found that another way to heal from his bad memories was to learn something from those experiences. Most people agree that you can learn from your unhappy memories. Psychologists call this rationalizing and even though it has a label from psychologists, rationalizing is not a bad thing.

If you've read my other books, *Heal Your Memories, Change Your Life* and *The Ultimate Guide To Healing Your Past*, you know that the man I've been describing is me. Fifty years ago, I was home sick from kindergarten. I was too sick to be up playing with toys so I entertained myself by looking at a calendar for the year 1966. I looked at each block for every day of that year and pictured what would be on television that night. I also imagined the opening tune for the show. For Saturday, for example, I imagined the dolphin Flipper and played "They call him Flipper, Flipper" in my head. By the end of that week, I had the entire calendar memorized for that year.

As the years continued and as each day went by, I made mental notes of what day it was. I now know every day for the past fifty years. This includes what the day of the week was, what the weather was like, and any significant news and personal events.

If you read *Heal Your Memories Change Your Life,* I taught you how to let go of the pain from unpleasant memories. Even if you don't remember as much as I do, I showed you that if you have painful memories, you can let go of the pain even if you can't let go of the memory. I offered many techniques that have worked time and again for my counseling clients. I included stories of amazing people who overcame challenges including bullying, head injuries, bad relationships, and childhood abuse. They all healed and now have happy and productive lives.

After compartmentalizing the memories into happy, unhappy, and mixed memories, I also found that you can learn from any memory to continue healing from your past. In *The Ultimate Guide To Healing Your Past,* I shared this technique with you. If you didn't already learn something from what happened to you before, you can look back and learn something now. You read about some more amazing people who learned from their unhappy memories in *The Ultimate Guide to Healing Your Past*, including a nurse who served in Vietnam during the war, an expert on false allegations of child abuse, and a woman who had a **defining moment** when she found that having animals in her life made her happy.

Now, I hope to teach you how to use your memories by turning them into defining moments to empower yourself. Defining moments or moments of empowerment are times when you did or could have turned your life around.

We have all had defining moments in our lives. Some are positive defining moments including whether or not you decided to get married or what career you wanted to pursue. People who suffer from addictions often say that their defining moment is when they decided to get help and go to a detox unit and rehab center when they hit rock bottom.

Hitting rock bottom is not limited to recovery from addictions. You can hit rock bottom when you decide you are not going to put up with an abusive partner or coworker. You can hit rock bottom when you have everything you ever wanted but are still unhappy and start singing the Peggy Lee song, "Is that All There Is?" Any time you are dissatisfied with your life and feel helpless can be rock bottom.

You might think that my ability to remember every day for fifty years and still going would have been empowering enough, but this ability has not given me all of the tools that I needed to succeed in life. Using your memories, your experiences, and especially your rock bottom to empower yourself requires a conscious effort. Let me share with you some defining moments in my life where I consciously decided to use my experiences to empower myself to grow, achieve, and be happier.

One defining moment of my life happened during middle school. Seventh grade is a bundle of contradictions for most. Sometimes you still feel like a child but other times you feel like you are the most grown up person in the room. Sometimes you get emotional and even have crying spells and are unable to understand why you are suddenly so sad. Other times you feel good to the point where the feelings seem too intense to handle. When a twelve-year-old kid feels this way, they often cry out that they are feeling feelings that no one in the history of the world has ever felt, and of course no one else understands them.

Since seventh graders are so intense, they get offended easily and if a peer says the wrong thing to them, merciless bullying often ensues. I recall the day I committed social suicide. It was Monday, February 12, 1973. It was gym class and we were doing some gymnastics. The gym teachers opened the partition in the gym that day so the boys and the girls could interact. As I mounted the horse apparatus in the gym, there were two attractive and friendly girls standing there. One of them said that I did a good job clearing the horse. She then turned to her friend and said that she thought I would be very nice if I weren't so shy. We chatted for a minute and then they asked me why I didn't like girls. There were three girls in

15

my class that I liked, but I had been keeping it a secret because I thought I would be teased about it.

For some reason, I thought I would come across better if I teased them a little. I said, "Because they are stupid." Instead of laughing, they got mad and that was the beginning of constant bullying for me.

About a month later, on Friday, March 23, 1973, I told my parents how bad the bullying was. A couple of days later, on March 25, my father sat down and suggested that if I became the best student in my class that I would be more respected. I also received encouragement from my mother and my English teacher.

Three days later on Wednesday, March 28, my Spanish teacher commented to me during class that I looked confused. Later she said the same thing to another pupil and someone else in the class commented, "All the dumb kids look confused."

On Easter Sunday, April 22, my parents and I discussed at the dinner table the importance of getting a good job and how it would only happen if I had good grades in school and went to college. Two days later on Tuesday, April 24, the morning announcer gave a pep talk over the intercom: "We are in the home stretch – school is almost over for summer! Don't give up now."

As I pondered all of these events, I had a defining moment. I had always believed I was smart, but now I decided to consciously see myself as a good student and imagined how it would feel to learn more, get good test papers back, get the respect of my schoolmates, and succeed in life. I empowered myself to be a good student, and from then on I worked hard in school.

Perhaps surprisingly, I did get a reputation as a good student. My schoolmates were and are good people and now I have a lot of fun communicating with them on Facebook. My last reunion on Saturday, November 30, 2013, was a lot of fun.

Another defining moment for me was three years later, in the spring of 1976, when I was going through some teenage turmoil. It seems that every teenager goes through phases where they feel alone, that nobody understands them, and their self-esteem hits an all-time low. I was not depressed, I was just aggravated all the time. Occasionally I also felt anxious as the big high school was somewhat overwhelming. On Thursday, November 13, the band director told me I was so bad at playing the trumpet that I wasn't allowed to play anymore and I should just take attendance for the rest of the year. On Monday, December 15, the tryouts for the school production of *The Music Man* ended and I did not get a speaking part in the show even though I really wanted one. My nerves were so frazzled all the time that my grades dropped significantly.

Every day I felt aggravated. The only benefit I seemed to get was that by late in the day my body felt the pleasant sensation one might experience after a good workout. However, I knew I could get that same sensation by exercising for a half hour instead of feeling agitated all day.

One night in May of that year (I will not disclose the date for personal reasons), I decided I had enough and I empowered myself to take control of my emotions. I suddenly was able to let go of the aggravation. I felt a peace that I had never felt before. It seemed that I was connected to everything in the entire universe and I felt like everything was exactly as it was supposed to be. I felt a strong compassion towards everyone.

I adopted the belief that there are alternatives to feeling aggravated. I saw myself as someone who can control my feelings and experience peace, joy, and compassion. For the next few months, every time I felt an unwanted feeling such as anger, anxiety, or sadness, I decided to let it go and feel happy and peaceful. I felt so empowered knowing that I could control how I felt. I recall one of many instances where I affirmed to myself that I now had control over how I felt.

Friday, September 24, 1976, I was at a church retreat in Avalon, New Jersey. As the group took turns introducing themselves, one young lady forgot another person's name. She then shared how guilty she felt. I quickly reminded myself that guilt and any unhappy feelings are a choice. If I had forgotten the person's name, I would have chosen not to feel guilty.

Choosing not to feel guilty doesn't make me or anyone else a callous person. An additional observation I've made is to see that people do the best they can with what they have. Everyone seems to take the best actions they know to take in order to meet their needs. Understanding this has empowered me to feel compassionate and caring towards anyone I choose to.

Most people seem to care about their families and friends, and sometimes they stretch that temporarily to give to charity. It is as if their compassion and love are encapsulated in a bottle with a cork. Consequentially, our compassion for others can't go too far or include too many people. However, I learned how to pop the cork on my bottle and have empowered myself to care about anybody I choose to. Empowering yourself to be compassionate towards others and to care for them is true spirituality.

Some people seem to feel as if the idea of empowering yourself is not spiritual but prideful because they think they are taking matters into their own hands instead of acknowledging God and His power. However, I choose to believe that God allows us to experience certain things so that we can learn from those experiences and empower ourselves and push ourselves to be our better selves. God actually expects us to learn from the opportunities He presents us, and as we do, He will give us more power to succeed and further His will.

Furthermore, when we help others maybe by painting their house, picking them up from work because their car died, or helping them carry in the grocery bags from the car, or when we accomplish things, like a project at work or a dissertation for school, it makes us feel strong and empowered – this is a natural feeling. Some people also believe that God feels everything we feel, so while you feel accomplished and empowered by helping someone else of from accomplishing something, God must feel good, too.

There have been many times besides the memories I've shared with you already when I empowered myself to make my life better. My first few years after college were frustrating. I graduated from La Salle University on Sunday, May 16, 1982, with a Bachelor of Arts in Psychology. It was tough for college graduates to get a decent job after graduation in the early and mid-1980s and the next few years were filled with jobs in sheltered workshops and community living arrangements with emotionally taxing and low-paying work.

By mid-1986, I decided that the field of mental health and human services held nothing for me. On Monday, November 10, 1986, I started a job as an assistant manager in a security firm. On Monday, December 1, my boss sent me out for a week to do night shift as a security guard in a gear plant. On Tuesday, December 9, he called me into his office and told me that the office job I had been hired for was going to be eliminated and that I would continue being a guard instead. The next month was nothing but night shifts in a gear plant and a meat packing plant. I barely got to se

Not seeing my family over the holidays was the last straw. During the night shift on Wednesday, December 31, going into January 1, 1987, I decided this had to be a year of empowerment. Although I always believed I was smart, the desperate state of the job market in the 80s led me to operate under the belief that there were no good jobs available for people with a bachelor's degree. That night, instead of sulking about the job market, I empowered myself to do what I needed to do so that I could get a job I enjoyed. First I took an education course at the local community college and then I applied to graduate education programs. In the fall of 1987, I was accepted into the graduate education program at Temple University.

Part of empowering yourself is not listening to naysayers. Before applying to Temple, I had been accepted into an undergraduate education program. However, one day the Department Chair called me into her office and said I could not be a teacher because I did not seem professional enough. I asked her why I had been accepted in the first place but she evaded the question. After my acceptance into the graduate program at Temple, I wrote a letter to the dean of the school of the undergraduate education program and received a nice apologetic response for how I was treated. Note that another part of empowerment is not taking garbage from anyone.

I eventually changed schools and majors and my life has been better for it. I changed my field of study to Counseling Psychology at Chestnut Hill College but I still proved that I was professional enough to teach and have successfully taught college courses. First I changed my beliefs about what was possible, and then I saw myself as a successful teacher and counselor. I collected my confidence and made all of the necessary moves to make the changes.

This four-step formula is what I use to achieve my goals and also what I use to help my counseling and coaching clients to empower themselves. I have seen hundreds of people begin happier lives and achieve their goals using this technique. You can use this technique for any memory or any of your present circumstances where you feel helpless and disempowered. Let's look at each step-in detail and why it is important.

Example 1 – The Four Steps To Empowerment

1.   Step one is to change your beliefs. Beliefs are not facts, they are conclusions you have drawn about life. You have beliefs about yourself, other people, how the world works, what works in life, and what does not work in life. Although beliefs are not facts, they have a profound impact on how you live. For example, if you believe that you can't get a job or can't attract a partner you will either not try at all, or you will muster up all the willpower you can and you will have to force yourself to try because you do not believe that it will work. You will be like a car with the gas and the brakes on simultaneously.

When I was still a mediocre student, an angry young man, and an educated security guard, I turned my circumstances around by first changing my beliefs about what I could do and what was possible in the world. If I had not changed my beliefs first, the changes I needed to make in my life would have been much harder to make. Trying to do something when you don't believe it can be done will always feel like a heavy burden on your back.

Most people base their beliefs on their memories. If they had a bad experience or have failed at something in the past, they will assume they are going to fail at it again in the present so they don't bother trying. Others may adopt the belief that they can do what they need to do if they practice and learn how to do the skill correctly. Ever heard the expression *whether you believe you can or you can't, either way, you are right*? I truly believe that if you believe you can do something, then you will be able to do it. But, if you limit yourself and think that you can't do something, then you probably won't be able to do it. To empower yourself, you must first change your beliefs and align them with what it is you want to accomplish.

21

2. Step two is to see yourself as the kind of person you must be in order to achieve your goal. This step follows closely with changing your beliefs. You must imagine yourself doing the thing you want to do. Visualizing it may or may not be necessary. It depends on if you are good at visualizing. You do not have to sit in a quiet place and meditate, although that would be useful. If you don't want to meditate or visualize, it will help just think about what life will be like when you are empowered and try to feel the confidence you need to succeed.

I can recall a time when I imagined myself as a teacher and a counselor without actually sitting down and meditating. It was Wednesday, June 1, 1988. I was working with some clients in a supportive employment program. After we finished and I walked to my car, I started to imagine myself as a teacher and a counselor. I imagined myself performing the duties of those roles and enjoying them. For the next few months, I thought this way whenever I had a free moment.

3. Step three is to feel the feelings. For this step, you may not need to do anything in particular. Many of my clients have told me that when they change their beliefs and imagine the results, the confident feelings come naturally.

4. Step four is to take the appropriate actions. When you have completed the first three steps, the next logical thing to do is take action. Some people will do the first three steps but then not take action. They believe they are empowered, see themselves as empowered and feel it, but something stops them from taking action.

Now we'll do an exercise that will show you exactly how to use these four steps to empower yourself and succeed in your goals.

Exercise 1 – I Can Empower Myself

For this exercise, you will need a pen or pencil and paper, or you can use a computer application like Word.

1. **Think of a memory that bothers you. It doesn't have to be a major trauma, just try to think of a time when you felt that someone was making you angry, sad, or uncomfortable and you didn't have any power to change the situation. It might be a time a parent or an authority figure verbally or physically abused you and still demanded respect from you. It could be a time someone did not want to listen to you but insisted that you listen to them. Any memory that made you feel powerless will do.**

2. **Write down the memory with as much detail as you can remember.**

3. **Write what beliefs you developed from the memory on the left side of a clean sheet of paper. For example, do you now believe that you are worth less than other people or that your opinions don't matter? Do you believe that if anyone contradicts you then they are right and you are wrong? Do you believe you can have no effect on anything?**

4. **On the right side of the paper, think of a positive belief that contradicts the limiting belief you wrote on the left side. For example, if you wrote, *my opinion does not count, no one will ever take me seriously*, the contradicting statement could be, *this person in the memory did not take me seriously but others do and will.***

This person has their own issues and I shouldn't take it personally.

5. **Spend a few minutes thinking about the good empowering beliefs that you wrote. The longer you think about them, the more you will, pardon the pun, believe them.**

6. **Notice if you feel the confident and empowered feelings. If you don't feel more confident and empowered, ask yourself if you could feel that way if you allowed yourself to.**

7. **Write on your paper any actions you will now take in your life that you would not have taken before.**

Now that you have completed the first exercise, do you feel empowered? Notice how empowered you feel even though your circumstances are the same. Now you can feel more confident to change the aspects of your life that you are unhappy with. Although your external world has not changed, your internal world has. You can now take action to change your external world.

If you don't feel as empowered as you'd like to, you can go through the exercise as many times as you want with the same memory until you are satisfied. As I shared earlier in my story from 1988 when I imagined myself as a teacher and a counselor, I too wasn't ready to take action the first time I went through the exercise. Also, I have found through my experience with clients that they seem to have the most trouble with the first step. If you find yourself hesitant to take the actions necessary to achieve your goals, you may need to go back to step one. Think about any beliefs you might have that would keep you from taking action and becoming empowered. Perhaps you have mixed feelings about achieving the goal. In this case, you would need to start over with step one and change the beliefs that are causing your mixed feelings. Identifying all of the beliefs that you have regarding a certain memory can take time, and you might need some practice.

Also, if you've never spent time visualizing before, this can seem strange. Essentially, if you had any trouble with the exercise, practicing it a few times will help to make it more effective.

Many clients feel awkward when they first go through the exercise. Anything that is new seems strange and awkward. If you are out of shape and start an exercise program that can certainly feel awkward at first. Understandably, if you are not used to changing your beliefs or imagining and feeling that you are someone you currently are not, then this exercise might be uncomfortable for you in the beginning. A part of you might feel that this is silly. Next, we'll discuss some reasons why you might hesitate to go through the steps I've outlined, and ways to help you get through them anyway.

Chapter 2 QR Code

http://www.phenomenalmemory.com/BookResources/video3.htm

Chapter 2

Clearing the Roadblocks to Achieving Self-Empowerment

If you completed the first exercise and successfully felt empowered to achieve a goal or to reclaim the power you may have lost from a past experience then congratulations! You are on your way towards total self-empowerment.

However, if you felt uncomfortable or like the exercise didn't work for you, there could be several reasons. Let's look at the possible reasons why it did not seem to work.

You may have had a problem with the first step. Many people are so used to basing their beliefs on their past experiences that it seems surreal to adopt a belief that they have no evidence for. However, take a look around and notice whether or not there are other people who can do things that you can't seem to do.

Frank, are you trying to make me angry? Why do that? Well, I asked you to do this to illustrate that the reason most people are able to accomplish things is simply that they believe they can. The more you focus on something and believe something, the more you will incorporate it into your life.

Instead of being jealous of other peoples' accomplishments, see those accomplishments as proof that something is possible even for you. For example, perhaps you know someone who is more assertive than you are. You can observe them, learn from them, and see how it is that they are so assertive. What do they do differently from you? Once you've observed and studied that person, then you can do what they do but adjust it to your own demeanor.

Suppose though that you are four feet, five inches tall and fifty years old. Does observing Lebron James while he plays basketball and studying all his moves mean that you will play in the NBA and be as good as he is? Of course not, so you should also really consider: for what purpose do you want to accomplish your goal? You may discover that your real motive is simply to get in shape and be admired. You don't have to be Lebron James and you don't have to play basketball to have shapely muscles and godly endurance. Maybe you could join a local gym and start a fitness regimen and in this way, you could meet your true goals to be in shape and earn respect for your discipline and hard work.

Most people underachieve in some way. For years I underachieved academically in school and professionally in low-paying and under-challenging jobs. Then I went to graduate school and began advancing in the counseling profession. I believed growing up and even into my college years that there would never be any use for my special knowledge of the calendar and my ability to remember every day of my life since age six. Sure, I took action but only after I cemented the belief in myself that I could make better use of my talents. You too can empower yourself to use your skills and talents if you learn to believe that you can.

Exercise 2 – Removing The Blocks
You will need a pen and paper, or your Word document. You will also need everything you wrote down from Exercise 1.

1.   Pick a memory that made you feel that you were not as good or talented as you used to be. Feel free to use the same memory from Exercise 1, especially if you struggled with it.

2.   Write all of the beliefs you have about yourself, other people, and the world at large due to that memory. Write them on the left side of the paper.

3.   Now write a belief that challenges those beliefs. Pick at least one challenging belief for each disempowering belief that you wrote.

4.   When you have completed the first three steps, repeat Exercise 1. Notice if the goal or dream seems more real now.

5.   If you still feel funny about the exercise, think about whether or not there are any other beliefs that may be holding you back.

The second problem you may have had with the exercise is that when you tried to feel the feelings, nothing happened. Maybe you just couldn't conjure up any emotion. Maybe you feel there's no point or that it isn't appropriate because, in reality you haven't actually accomplished the goal you envisioned. Many people believe that their emotions are out of their control and that they can't feel something about a situation unless they are in that situation at that very moment. This roadblock can be overcome though once you see that we have been sold an untruth all of our lives. The untruth is that our feelings just happen to us in reaction to what is happening around us. The truth is that we are actually conditioned from an early age to feel certain things depending on the circumstances. For example, we are taught to be happy when we are on vacation, to be sad at a funeral, and to be angry when we do not get what we want.

Did you ever notice that not everyone reacts to the same situation with the same feelings? Let's take the classic example of a traffic jam. Some people sit in their car and sing along to the music on their MP3 player or car radio. Others make motions with their hands as if that could magically make the traffic move. Some people will fume silently while others will make a phone call while they are stopped. There are even some who curse and make offensive gestures with their fingers. All of these people are in the same situation but they react differently to their circumstances.

Even a funeral does not always have to produce sadness. If you read *Heal Your Memories, Change Your Life,* I told a story about how my Uncle Frank made me laugh at my grandfather's funeral. Many funerals today are celebrations of the person's life. They have a table with pictures of the person, their library card, maybe some artwork that they did, and other memorabilia. Funerals tell stories of the person's life.

There is no one set way to feel and behave for any situation. If you recall the time when you first fell in love, you probably had no qualm about feeling happy and distracted in the classroom or at a business meeting even though that may not have been the most appropriate emotion for the circumstance. So, even though you may have not actually accomplished the goal that you imagined in the exercise, it is still perfectly fine to feel like you have.

Another roadblock that I often see in my clients is that they feel like they are losing touch with reality and the whole exercise is nothing but fantasy. If you are a rational, well-grounded adult, you too may feel strange imagining and feeling that you have accomplished something that is not part of concrete reality. However, spending time in your own imagination is actually good for you!

It is healthy and good for your well-being to spend an average of ten minutes out of every hour lost in your own head with your imagination and the rest of the time being present and mindful of your concerns and surroundings. If you are working and don't have ten minutes every hour to spare, prioritize some time after you get home to just think and concentrate on what is going on in your own head as you garden or crochet. An hour is ideal, but any amount of time you can spare will be helpful.

Given that spending time in your own head is actually good for you, it follows that you will not lose touch with reality if you spend some time during the exercise feeling and imagining that you have achieved something that you haven't really achieved yet.

Once you are finished with the exercise, you can and will go back to the real world and tend to your affairs.

Another reason you may resist empowerment is that maybe you are afraid that someone might not like the changes you make. Maybe you are in a marriage or a relationship with someone who is controlling and if you empower yourself to stand up to them or become so successful that you don't need them anymore, naturally they will not like that. However, the reason you want to empower yourself is that you feel powerless and this controlling relationship could very well be part of the reason you feel powerless in the first place.

Many people live in an emotional prison that they unconsciously keep themselves in. They never get excited about anything, or they are always upset or angry. The question is: why would anyone want to live this way? Most of the time, it is because the person thinks they will be able to avoid disappointment if they never allow themselves to be happy. If they expect the worst and it happens then they are already prepared, and if something better happens they will be pleasantly surprised. However, living this way puts the person in a state of constant disappointment. They may never experience any happy moments.

If you recognize yourself in that description, it could be that you do not want to be empowered because you fear disappointment. You might be thinking, *what if it doesn't work? What if I change my beliefs, pretend, feel, and try, and nothing happens?* If that is your question then I will respond with a question. When should you give up? Even if nothing happens the first time or the second time or even the third time, you can still keep working towards empowering yourself and reaching your goal. Most successful people in the world have tried and tried and tried again before they succeeded. Let's look at Abraham Lincoln as an example. First, he failed as a storekeeper. Then, when he wanted and tried to become the Illinois Game Warden, the people

31

who knew him laughed at him. He was not elected to the Senate, his first wife, Anne Rutledge, died young, and he lost two sons in childhood. Despite these failures and misfortunes, he is now regarded as one of the most successful presidents of the United States. So, never give up and keep trying!

So now we have covered some difficulties that you might experience in steps one, two, and three of the exercise. **Practicing the steps will make the exercise progressively easier and more comfortable, and it will also change your internal world.** Step four is unique because it changes your external world.

In the previous chapter, we discussed how futile it can be to take action without believing that it will work or that you can succeed. It's kind of like when you were a newly licensed driver and you wondered why the car was not going fast even when you put the pedal to the metal only to discover that you still had the parking brake on. Taking action without changing your beliefs, imagining your accomplishment, and feeling the accomplished feelings makes you a walking car with the gas pedal and the brake pedal on at the same time.

There is a common tendency for people to not understand why things seem to come so easily to other people but so difficult for themselves. Perhaps you are someone who feels that you put forth effort but then you doubt your ability and think that you won't get any results no matter how hard you try. Completing steps one through three of the exercise could make your efforts less difficult and the action you take might come as a breeze like they appear to when you see other people trying the same thing.

Perhaps you are on the opposite end of the spectrum – a dreamer. You have no trouble believing that you can do something better than you remember doing it in the past, but then you struggle to take action as detailed in step four.

Part of performing step four successfully is that you need to associate enough pleasure with taking action while also associating enough pain with not taking action. If you believe you can do something, imagine doing it, and feel the victorious feeling but then follow all that up by going to the kitchen and grabbing some chips to munch on while you watch the latest episode of *Keeping Up with the Kardashians,* then you will not develop the pleasant association between what you imagined and actually accomplishing what you imagined. The best time to take action is immediately after you do the first three steps. I'll give you a personal example.

Some of the best memories of my life have involved spending time at the New Jersey shore. The corollary of that is that some of my worst memories were thinking that I would never spend much time at the shore again.

One of the worst days of my life was Friday, August 4, 1978, when after spending a fifth summer with my family at the shore for the first seven weeks of the summer, I knew that tradition was ending. I wondered if I would ever get back to the shore for very long.

On Saturday, July 5, 1997, I was all packed up and had just handed my key in from spending a week at a condo with some friends in Sea Isle City, New Jersey. I was not ready to go home yet. I sat in a pavilion overlooking the ocean and thought about how much I would love to move to the shore area.

As I observed the beach that hot and sunny morning in 1997, I had a pen and paper, and I decided to change some of the beliefs that were keeping me from moving to the shore that I loved so much. The beliefs I decided to change were that I would never spend time at the shore again and also that the only kind of work available in the shore area was construction and tourism. I instead decided to believe that I could, in fact, find a counseling job offshore and commute. Then I imagined myself living there. Sitting on a wood pavilion watching people swim and sunbathe made it easy to imagine myself living there and enjoying it. For about a half hour, I created scenarios in my head about living there, including how I would live and what I would do. I felt very excited and the longer I visualized my life in that way, the more real it seemed.

Now with steps one through three completed, it was time for step four. Instead of starting right away on the two and a half hour journey back to Pennsylvania, I visited a realtor and looked at a couple of houses. Looking at houses right away helped me to associate actual pleasure with the goal I imagined myself achieving and helped to jump start my path to achieving my goal. The following Monday, I wrote a letter to the New Jersey State House, the capitol building in Trenton, New Jersey, for a listing of counseling jobs in the state. It took a few months but on Sunday, November 16, 1997, I moved to the shore and have been there ever since.

If you keep doing exercises one and two and still feel disempowered, you may need some professional coaching. You can visit my website at www.phenomenalmemory.com any time to schedule a consult with me.

In the next few chapters, you are going to read about some people who empowered themselves to become happy and successful, just like you can. All of the people in the next few chapters faced challenging memories of their past, and although they could have allowed their memories to make them bitter or angry, they overcame and empowered themselves to make the most of their lives and to help those around them. After you read these stories and are convinced that you also can empower yourself no matter what your memories contain, I'll then share some more details with you on what empowerment really is, and more ways you can apply it to your life.

Chapter 3 QR Code

http://www.phenomenalmemory.com/BookResources/video2.htm

Chapter 3

Use Your Naysayers and Your Supporters to Achieve Your Dream

Sunday, August 19, 1973 is a day that Claudio will never forget. This eight-year-old boy who loved Batman left his home for a day out with his uncle and discovered his passion in life.

Claudio's uncle worked at the Allegheny Club inside Three Rivers Stadium in Pittsburgh, Pennsylvania. This is the stadium where the city's professional baseball team, the Pirates, played. On this sunny Sunday, Claudio's uncle took him to the stadium for a day of bonding.

Inside the club, they saw pictures of baseball players, including Roberto Clemente who had been killed in a plane crash the previous New Year's Eve while flying supplies to Nicaraguan earthquake victims. After they left the club, they went into the locker room and saw the current team's players, including Al Oliver and Willie Stargell, joking around and playing cards. Then they went into the stands and on the field. Claudio was awestruck by everything.

That entire day changed the course of Claudio's life. Upon his return home, his dad, Olindo, first asked him, "Did you have a good time today at the game?" He replied, "I did, and I know now what I want to do with the rest of my life. I want to be in professional baseball!" His father responded, "If that is what you want to do then me and your Mom will do all we can to make your dreams come true." His mother chimed in with some additional encouragement and said, "If that's what you want, that's what we want. We love you."

Many years later, when Claudio was twenty-three, his mother died of stomach cancer. Claudio stood at the casket and felt so distraught that for the first time in fifteen years, he felt that he did not care about sports or living. Intuitively his father sensed this and said, "You can't quit, you are the only one left for her legacy."

Claudio did not always have the support of everyone. As he grew up playing ball and then also when he coached teams later on, his extended family constantly tried to discourage him. After his mother passed away, other family members seized the opportunity to talk some sense into Claudio, or so they thought. One relative told him, "It is time to quit baseball, grow up, and be a man." Another told him, "Now it's really time to grow up." Claudio took the comments harshly. He had just lost his mother and the rest of his family was telling him to give up his dream, too. The family members who said negative things to him were not trying to talk sense into him, and they were not trying to help him or protect him. For whatever selfish reason, they just didn't want him to accomplish his dreams.

Claudio's naysayers extended beyond his family. His first coaching position was at Quaker Valley High School for the school's baseball team. The former coach of the team actually used to throw grapes at Claudio during games in an effort to distract him and make it difficult for him to lead his team to win. Another coach for the school treated Claudio in such a way that it stripped him of his confidence in his ability to coach.

Eventually, Claudio left his first coaching position because of all the negativity and harassment. After that, he found it difficult to find another coaching position. He wrote to over one hundred and fifty professional teams and colleges looking for a job, but he was turned down or ignored. Finally, he was hired by Quigley Catholic High School as an assistant head coach for a salary of eight hundred dollars a year. His father was quick to encourage him and told him, "Even though this is not where you want to be, you treat this job as if you were coaching the Yankees. I am proud of you."

In November of 1999, Claudio called James Gamble of the Global Scouting Bureau (GSB), an organization that helps professional athletes obtain contracts. Claudio continued to call James once a month for the next year until James finally offered Claudio the job of Professional Baseball Scout in January of 2001. In 2002, Claudio was promoted to General Manager and Professional Scout of the GSB.

In 2005, Claudio received a call from Carnegie Mellon University to offer him the head coaching position for the university's baseball team. He accepted their offer and has been at Carnegie ever since.

In 2011, Claudio was voted into the Carnegie Mellon University Baseball Hall of Fame. In that same year, Claudio received the Willie Stargell MVP Lifetime Achievement Award. In 2014, he was voted into the Steel City Sports World Hall of Fame. The former Pirate player Al Oliver was inducted with him. Claudio and Al have become friends and they play golf together.

Claudio is still the current head baseball coach at Carnegie, and he still scouts for GSB. On top of those two full-time activities, he also co-hosts a sports-based reality television show called *Steel City Sports*. He has even been invited to the Swing FORE Sickle Cell Celebrity Golf Outing, an annual event that helps to raise awareness for children living with sickle cell anemia.

You could say that Claudio's story is the American Dream in more ways than one. He endured naysayers, he endured abuse, and he endured heartache but he always stuck to his dream of a career in baseball. Claudio used his supporters and his naysayers to empower himself. After his mother passed away, his father continued to support him and he drew heavily on that support for strength and empowerment. As for his naysayers, he determined that he was not going to let them see him fail and this also empowered him to achieve many great things. He says to anyone pursuing a

dream, "You will be hurt, knocked down, depressed, discouraged at times. But you really do have to get back up, dust yourself off and go right back at it! It is as simple as that. Either you fight, or you do not. You have to want it." Claudio had persistence, faith, and hard work, and he empowered himself to make his dream his reality.

Some people do not have the encouragement that Claudio had from their parents. In the next chapter, you will read about a man who had to learn to heal bad memories of his childhood at home and empower himself to forgive and help others.

Chapter 4 QR Code

http://www.phenomenalmemory.com/BookResources/video5.htm

Chapter 4

Achieve Peace in Forgiveness

Steve's hardships began when he incredibly young. At the age of two, he contracted polio and the disease affected his mind such that he can't remember anything of his life prior to the age of six. Polio though was only the beginning of his challenges.

Steve was raised in a military family. His father fought in World War II and also did a tour in the Korean War. After all the fighting and horrible things his father had seen on his tours, he came home with Post-traumatic Stress Disorder (PTSD). Steve's mother also developed PTSD from the stress and hardships of being a military man's wife.

Life at home was stressful for everyone. Steve's father would have panic attacks which led him to be physically abusive to Steve and his siblings, including frequently smacking them on their heads. His father was also verbally abusive. Steve recalls an incident when he was ten years old and his brother was about to get into a street fight with another boy. Steve's father, drunk and on the verge of a panic attack, came out and punched his son, Steve's brother, so hard that his head swelled when it hit the concrete. They did not take Steve's brother to the hospital because it would have ruined his father's military career. His brother sustained a traumatic brain injury without medical intervention. On another occasion, Steve's father came home in a panic and crushed a salt shaker and smashed a toilet. Because of these incidents, Steve and his siblings learned to hold their hands over their heads to protect themselves when their father was around.

Steve's contempt and anger towards his father continued throughout much of his adult life. His father died in 1998 when Steve was in his early fifties. Steve did not attend the funeral.

Around the time of his father's funeral, Steve realized he needed to heal his past. First, he moved away from the stress of his work and into a log cabin with his family in Leavenworth, Washington. He quit drinking and developed healthy eating habits. In 2005, Steve decided to move to Oregon and continue to try to heal from his traumatic childhood.

Steve began to study PTSD and how it gets passed down intergenerationally. He entered therapy and learned mindfulness techniques. These are therapeutic techniques that teach the client to focus on the present moment. It helps because the client will not focus on past trauma nor worry about the future. Steve also began learning and sharing about PTSD. He started writing blog posts which evolved into books. Through writing, Steve developed a deeper understanding of the how's and why's of what happened to him growing up and he was able to use these experiences to help others. His deeper understanding and his ability to help others empowered Steve to eventually forgive his father for the horror he put Steve and his family through.

Steve has now written four books about his past and how he has healed. He gives speeches and writes blogs to help educate people about PTSD. His biggest focus is on children as he believes they are the ones who can and need to be helped the most.

Steve's life proves that you can heal even the most abusive memories. Our next chapter will share stories of two women who empowered themselves through memories of being physically ill.

Chapter 5 QR Codes

http://www.phenomenalmemory.com/bookresources/video19.htm

http://www.phenomenalmemory.com/bookresources/video20.htm

Chapter 5

A Debilitating Illness became an Empowering Illness

When Daisy was a child, she started to have seizures at unpredictable times. The seizures were caused by Unverricht-Lundborg disease, a rare inherited form of epilepsy. Having a rare disease in childhood is never easy, but because Daisy showed no outward physical signs of illness, no one around her seemed to understand that she was sick. She wasn't granted any special treatment at school to accommodate her illness, and her home life wasn't any gentler.

Daisy's mother was only sixteen years old when she had Daisy and was not prepared for motherhood. There was little warmth or nurturing and her mother berated her and hit her frequently.

Despite the recurring and unpredictable seizures, as well as the abusive and non-supportive home environment, Daisy went to college and made her life a success. She even went so far as to start her own lucrative public relations firm.

Daisy's life seemed to be moving along well until one day when she was in a near-fatal car accident. She was knocked unconscious for four minutes. After the accident, she was hospitalized for quite a while but her parents didn't come to visit her at all even though she had just had a near-death experience.

The accident turned out to be quite a spiritual experience for Daisy as it caused her to begin questioning her life's purpose. When she returned to work, she suddenly found public relations boring. She wanted to do something more meaningful with her life. Daisy realized her main supporters were in Los Angeles, California, so she moved there from London. She is now heavily involved in charity work, as well as fashion design, including fashion designs for some top movie stars.

Daisy has used all of her experiences and memories to empower herself. She used the near-death experience in the car accident to see her life as meaningful. Then she used her illness along with her childhood abuse to see her purpose of advocating for human rights. As a now confident woman, she has begun applying to some of the top law schools in the country to fulfill her heart's desire to advocate for ill and abused people as an attorney.

Daisy's story is quite inspirational. She overcame childhood illness and abuse and a near death experience and saw those experiences as a means to propel her life into a greater purpose. This next story is about another woman who also overcame an illness and empowered herself through her experience of being sick.

Amy was a talented young girl. One of her many talents was a great singing voice and she nurtured this talent by taking voice lessons in high school. One of the benefits of the voice lessons was that she thought she had made a great friend in her teacher. He cared about her on a personal level even to the point of offering to be her personal mentor and godfather. However, one day all of the trust Amy had for him was shattered when he molested her. This experience left her feeling betrayed and hurt, and she was completely confused.

People hold tension in different parts of their body and Amy was no exception. Although Amy's family was supportive, any expression of unhappy feelings was not encouraged and she often felt that she was not permitted to express herself. Because she wasn't able to express her feelings, she held her tension in her stomach which often felt tight after she experienced being sexually abused by her teacher. Almost a year after the incident and a few days after her eighteenth birthday, her stomach actually exploded due to a blood clot.

Amy almost died and was dependent on life support for a long time. There was no certainty that she was going to live. It would be about six years before she could actually eat food instead of being fed intravenously. Years of physical therapy began where she had to relearn to walk and talk. Amy endured twenty-seven surgeries before everything was said and done. The fact that she lived at all was called a medical miracle by the press.

When Amy was discharged from the hospital, her family took her to a lawyer. The lawyer, however, advised Amy that a court battle would be too much stress for her physically and emotionally and she needed to heal first. Given her upbringing and the lack of emotion typically expected by her family, Amy found it interesting that her parents didn't want to keep her experience of abuse a secret and that they went public with a lawyer.

For years following her hospitalization, every-day living presented many triggers for Amy's anxiety and anger. For example, being strapped into a car seat reminded her of being confined in the hospital and strapped to an IV pole. She also often had episodes of dissociation and derealization. Dissociation is when current circumstances are stressful to the point that they cause a person to disconnect from their current reality. Derealization is slightly different and is when a person doesn't believe or feel like their surroundings are real – they feel like they aren't even in their own body anymore. Both of these psychological states served Amy as a defense mechanism – they helped her to guard herself against feeling too much pain during experiences that triggered memories of her past.

Amy tried to stay active. It seemed to her that if she stayed in one place and had too much down time in her own body and mind, the flashbacks worsened. She also tried to avoid anything too stimulating. Other beliefs she had included:
- If I don't keep moving, I will feel awful emotions.
- I cannot pause to look at anything. If I do, I'll remember awful things.
- I must keep doing, and I must always know what I am doing.
- I get a nervous feeling inside if I am in a small space.
- When my body feels pain, I am in surgery.
- I cannot stop moving. If I do, I will drown.
- If I go outside, I will feel too much and it will hurt too much.

Eventually, Amy decided that she did not want to live this way. She started journaling her thoughts and feelings and facing them. She looked at the process as self-soothing. The inspiration to journal came from a support group she attended at The National Alliance on Mental Illness or NAMI. This organization provides support groups and literature focused on mental illness. She realized that she was experiencing PTSD and it was completely normal after what she had been through.

Soon Amy discovered that even though writing helped her to face her feelings, it wasn't enough for her so she also began expressing herself through art and music. She wrote a one-woman musical about her life, painted it, sang it, yelled it, mourned over it, and finally accepted her condition. She now goes all over the country and performs the musical at colleges. Today, Amy not only performs her musical, she also writes freelance articles for the Huffington Post, gives speeches, acts, and writes plays.

Amy now says she feels that she did not have a choice but to keep going. These are her words to her tormentor: "You are my art, my story, my growth, my lesson learned. You are not my secret. Your secret will keep you sick." Rather than relinquishing power to a former abuser, Amy's words are a great tool to use to empower yourself.

Illness, of course, isn't the only kind of memory that we can use to empower ourselves. The next chapter shares a story of a man who found himself homeless, but instead of giving up, he empowered himself to create his best life.

Chapter 6 QR Code

http://www.phenomenalmemory.com/BookResources/video7.htm

Chapter 6

All Problems are Still Temporary

In my previous book, The Ultimate Guide to Healing Your Past, I interviewed Richard London, a man who has lived his life with the philosophy that all problems are temporary. Problems will persist until you decide to do something about them.

David Everett is a prime example of this philosophy. He had an experience that empowered his future.

David was a confident young 21-year-old man who lived in New York City with aspirations to become an actor. He had decided that college was not necessary at that time and worked in a hotel while he auditioned for various roles.

The hotel management changed David's shift from day to an overnight audit role. After a couple of months on the night shift David felt stressed and tired. He requested to be moved to one night shift a week and the rest of his shift on days. However, the manager disagreed and unceremoniously terminated his employment.

At the time, David was renting a room from an elderly woman. After two months of unsuccessful job hunting he had no money for rent. So, he packed up and moved his belongings to a storage shed and left.

With less than $100.00 in his pocket he checked into a homeless shelter. On the first night, David heard a man loudly cursing. When he looked to see what was going on, he saw the man had a knife in his hand. David became frightened and decided it was best to leave the shelter.

David's home became the streets of Manhattan. He subsisted on free water and raw Raman Noodles. He slept on a park bench in Riverside Park, close to where he previously lived. Every day he walked the streets of Manhattan. First, he showered and changed at a gym where he was a member. Then he went to Fed Ex and printed resumes on which us used a fake address.

Ironically, David had connections and knew people he could call who would have given him lodging. The problem was that his stepfather had always told him that you provided for yourself when you turned 18.

After a month on the streets, it seemed that David's luck was about to end. Then, one day, he walked into a retail store where he spotted someone he knew. It was an ex-supervisor from a previous job at a place called Club Monaco. Dan was happy to see David and immediately hired him to work at the store.

Since David now had a job and could pay rent, he felt better about living with a friend. So, he contacted Brandon, who took him in.

Understandably, David now sees that episode in his life as his "rock bottom." It is the same as when addicts feel they have hit rock bottom. They've lost everything and come to the realization that they must change. The addiction cost them everything so now they must get help.

David eventually enrolled in college and now has a degree. He currently runs his own consulting company and has worked in corporate America. It is now almost seven years since David has been homeless. He has empowered himself by learning to appreciate life.

It is useful to look back on the period of life that may have been your low point. Then you can feel grateful for everything you have that you lacked then. Let's do an exercise on this.

Exercise 3. Your Temporary Rock Bottom

You will need a pen and paper or word processing document.

> 1. *Think of a time in your life that could have been your worst. It could be a time when you were being abused, when your needs were not met, when you were depressed or anxious, etc.*
> 2. *Write everything you did not like about that time. List everything you may have felt depressed or angry about.*

3.   Write about what changed to end that bad time.

4.   What did you do to improve things?

5.   What did others do to help you?

6.   How did or how can you empower yourself from what happened at that time? What skills do you have now? What are you now grateful for? How did you turn the negative into a positive?

Congratulations on completing this exercise! You are well on your way to total empowerment!

If you believe the memory you used for this exercise wasn't significant or dramatic, you aren't alone in that thinking. Most people feel their memories are not that dramatic. Even if that is true, the memories are still important.

In the next chapter, you will read about two young women who not only overcame rape, but who recognize the experience took their lives in directions they might not have gone otherwise.

Chapter 7 QR Code

http://www.phenomenalmemory.com/BookResources/video8.htm

Chapter 7

Support is Empowering: No One Heals Alone

One night, in 2000, Kelley was walking home from her job in a local restaurant in Chicago, Illinois. Suddenly, a man jumped out of an alley, grabbed her, pinned her down, and shoved his fist inside her dress. Fortunately, Kelley had recently taken a self-defense course and she knew what to do. She looked him straight in the eye, kicked him as hard as she could, ran to the nearest bar, and asked them to call the police.

For the next two weeks, Kelley called out of work. She was terrified to leave her house. She started to fall behind in her schoolwork. Finally, she had enough and decided she needed to resume her life. However, she knew she could not do that without help, so she entered group and individual therapy. Since the assault happened away from her job they would not pay for the therapy. She had to pay herself.

In her women's support group, she learned that some of the other women had also been assaulted in the same location. Kelley was not aware of this until she joined the group.

Kelley was fortunate to have a boyfriend who was very supportive. He stayed with her through all her fears, crying spells, and angry outbursts. Paradoxically, her therapists and group members told her he probably would not stay with her based on statistics from other rape victims. However, her man was steadfast and she eventually married him.

Although the therapy helped her, Kelley credits the support of her husband as the main reason she became empowered to move past the assault trauma. Kelley continued her education and became a social worker, married her loving boyfriend, and had four children.

Most people who have traumatic memories have had more than one traumatic experience. In high school Kelley battled anorexia. Anorexia is a disease where the person has an exaggerated image of their body and voluntarily starves themselves. After the birth of each child she suffered from postpartum depression. This is where the new mother becomes depressed for several weeks to several months after the birth of her baby. Alcoholism and drug addiction run in her family. Kelley struggled with alcohol addiction in recent years but has now been sober for three years. The support of her husband and groups has helped with that, as well.

Today, Kelley has an eclectic counseling practice, called *Serendipitous Psychotherapy*. Her life experience led her to call it "serendipitous" as she sees how all the trials in her life made her a good counselor.

In my own practice, when I counsel people with PTSD, the goal is to reach a happy medium of vigilance. When a client first experiences a trauma they are often hypervigilant to the point where they are afraid to live, as Kelley was for the first two weeks after the assault. PTSD can occur after a car accident where the person becomes afraid to drive. It includes people who were hurt in an accident and people who hurt someone else. Sometimes, it is not that severe. When the car spun out of control they were scared and they suddenly realize they can't control as many things in their life as they believed they could. That is a terrifying thought for some people.

When the patient starts therapy, they express their fear of driving, if they were involved in a car accident, or, in the case of a rape, leaving the house. Throughout the course of therapy, they empower themselves, they learn relaxation exercises, and cognitive techniques to change their thoughts. Cognitive

therapy consists of changing thoughts and beliefs. I think of it as a rail train with three stops--Thought Factory, Feeling Junction, and Behavior Arrival.

Thought Factory is where you change your thoughts and beliefs. For example, if you believe you are an easy target for abuse or rape, you change that thought to one that confirms you can handle and protect yourself. Then, when you arrive at Feeling Junction, you notice that you are not as afraid as you used to be. Behavior Arrival is the point where you go out more and begin to resume your life.

Kelley shared that, since the assault, she is more vigilant to potential danger than before, but not to the point of panic or disabling anxiety. She has found a happy medium for living her life, which she teaches to her children.

***

While Kelley was attacked on the street, this next story is of a woman who was attacked in her own home.

Sande has always been a lady with many talents. She learned to play the piano at the tender age of three and the violin at age four. She loved the violin and kept playing all through school. She even earned a music scholarship for her violin playing. All she had to do was re-audition to maintain the scholarship.

One late summer night, she lay in her bed at home. It was a few nights before she was to return to school for the audition to keep the music scholarship. The windows were open in her house and there was no alarm. Suddenly, she couldn't breathe. She was suffocating and she felt like she was dying. An intruder, carrying a knife had, broken into the house. He had covered her face, and was smothering her! She struggled, and managed to get out from under the pillow. She saw the knife, and quickly pulled it away away, wounding her left hand in the

process. She kicked her attacker in the stomach. She screamed as loudly as she could as he fled through the side door.

As she called the police, her brother walked in. The police happened to be right outside on the street and the arrived almost immediately. Apparently, there had been other intrusions in the neighborhood and the police were on guard. Ironically, they did not see the intruder enter the house or escape. He was never caught.

Sande's hand was bleeding and they took her to the hospital.

Since Sande had deep injuries in her left hand, she could no longer play the violin. She lost her scholarship. For a long time, she could not listen to classical music because it reminded her of her loss.

Sande did return to college. In fact, she has earned various degrees from several colleges, including MIT and the London School of Economics. She is a writer and video game designer. At one point, she was nominated for a Writers Guild of America Award for Achievement in Video Game Writing.

For a while after the assault she checked locks all the time. She took up writing to express herself, as she did not like to talk about the incident. Later, a friend experienced a sexual assault that went to trial.

When I asked Sande what kept her going and achieving things. The incident made her a stronger person. She had many things she still wanted to do and achieve before age 30 and the fact that she lives made her more determined to strive for what she wanted.

Her book, *Serious Games: Games That Educate, Train, and Inform,* can be purchased at Amazon.com.

Chapter 8 QR Code

http://www.phenomenalmemory.com/BookResources/video9.htm

Chapter 8

You can Empower yourself, whether your Traumatic Memories are from Childhood or Adulthood

Alceen seemed to find violence wherever she went. It started with her father, who verbally abused her as a child and seemed to think it was acceptable to do so. Alceen describes that the abuse made her feel like an ant, and she believed that her father knew just the right words to say to be hurtful.

The additional abuse came later from her cousin who molested her. Given her experiences, it is no surprise that Alceen had low self-esteem. The harsh words from her father and the abuse by her cousin played repeatedly in her head.

Children are taught to trust adults no matter what the adult does to them. Consequentially, Alceen did not feel encouraged to tell other adults that she was being abused. Holding the anger in makes it seem that the only choice for an abused child is to accept it and think of it as normal. Although Alceen did not accept the abuse, it still affected her life.

When Alceen started dating, she was involved in two relationships that included domestic abuse. She eventually found a good man to marry, and it was a good marriage until her husband became ill. In July of 2015, his foot became infected and the doctors had to amputate his little toe. He went into a rehabilitation facility but died in September of the same year.

In my book, Heal Your Memories, Change Your Life, I wrote about what forgiveness is and is not. Alceen learned through her experiences that we decide when we forgive someone. We do not have to wait until they say they are sorry or own what they did. This is an essential concept to grasp in life because it puts us in the driver's seat of forgiveness.

Eventually, Alceen empowered herself to set boundaries and make better choices. She forgave her dad, even when he did not confess to the abuse. Another way her memories empowered her was to show her that the example her father set for her as a parent was not one she would follow while raising her own children. She used her father as a non-role model for how to parent and instead of copying his abusive example she was going to treat her children with appropriate respect and courtesy.

Therapy and medication helped Alceen handle the loss of her husband. She still feels sad at times but is grateful that he is no longer in pain. She dwells more often on the good memories of him than on the sadness of loss.

When someone experiences loss, they typically go through specific stages of mourning. The first stage is denial. When someone experiences a loss and for the next day or two they say they can't believe how well they are handling it, they are probably at the stage of denial. At this stage, the sense of loss has not penetrated their consciousness.

Stage two is anger. The bereaved can feel angry at the doctors and nurses for not taking care of their loved one. They can be angry at the person they lost if they believe they did not take good care of themselves or were in some way to blame for what happened. For example, if they hadn't eaten so poorly, smoked, or drank, they might have lived longer. Sometimes they get angry with God for taking their loved one, especially if they judge the age of death to be too early.

When the bereaved person realizes that getting angry doesn't help anything, they move to stage three which is bargaining. At this stage, they do things that might seem irrational or neurotic. When they are alone in the house they might talk to the person as if they were standing right next to them, or they might write them a letter. If you know someone who is going through the bargaining phase, don't chastise them for doing things like this. It is part of the mourning process that they need to get through to be able to heal.

The fourth stage of mourning is the way we typically think of mourning – sadness and depression. The bereaved person cries feels sad, and may even become depressed.

Finally, stage five is acceptance. At this stage, the person has accepted their loss. The bereaved will know they have reached the stage of acceptance when they think of the person they've lost and feel more joy that they knew the person and had them in their life rather than feeling sadness because they are gone.

A person who experiences loss will typically vacillate between the stages. They do not finish one stage one day and start the next stage the next day. Similarly, you cannot plan your mourning. Alceen is now at the last stage in the mourning process most of the time – acceptance – although sometimes she returns to the mourning stage. It typically takes a year to get to the final stage of acceptance, but Alceen empowered herself so vehemently that it took her a shorter time.

Today, Alceen is a member of the Domestic Violence Speakers Bureau in her home town. She speaks about all aspects of domestic violence, including what it is like for the abused and the abuser. She also takes part in conducting workshops for survivors of domestic abuse which includes art therapy for another organization called Pearls for Creative Healing.

For some people like Alceen, trouble seems to follow them around. However, when you have the skills and knowledge to empower yourself, the level of your empowerment will grow with your trouble. In other words, the more often you see your troubled memories as opportunities to empower yourself, the easier it will be to kindle empowerment in your life and the more effective it will be.

Like Alceen, April was also sexually abused by a family member. Life for April while she was growing up was filled with fear, shame, and guilt. From the age of nine to nineteen, she was raped repeatedly by her stepfather. At one point, she even had a child by him. If that was not painful enough, she then had to give up her first child for adoption.

Many people who have been raped are afraid to tell anyone because the abuser threatens them. They threaten to kill them, hurt them, or hurt or kill a loved one. For April, her stepfather threatened to hurt her mother if April told anyone what he was doing to her.

April was angry at the people who did not protect her. Children expect to be protected. If they are hurt by an adult, they may have impulses to return the abuse, but of course, children are not physically able to do so. Instead, abused children will often turn their angry impulses inwards which often develop into an unhealthy sense of guilt. Abused children often feel that whatever horrible thing is happening to them, they must have brought it on themselves.

Shame is more personal than guilt. When a person experiences guilt, they believe and feel that they have done something wrong. They made a mistake. When a person experiences shame, however, the person believes they themselves are a mistake. Shame can and often does result in suicide.

Although April lived with feelings of guilt and shame, she found the strength to keep going. She fared well in school, studied engineering, and landed a high paying job at Intel, a multinational semiconductor manufacturing company. She chose engineering because her family told her, "That's where the money is."

April continued to live in fear even after her stepfather was incarcerated. Even though he was in jail, he still managed to make death threats against April, and she had to get an escort when taking college classes at night.

While April was preparing for her stepfather's court trial and to hopefully obtain some justice for the years of abuse he put her through, she met the man of her dreams. They got married and started a family all while continuing her demanding corporate job at Intel. She was now in her thirties and everything seemed to be going in the right direction.

Memorial Day of 2010 started out like any other holiday for April and her family, until her husband began sweating and breathing hard. They called an ambulance and rushed him to the hospital. Once they got into the emergency room, the staff called a "Code Blue." By the end of the day, April's husband had died. This was the day the spark was ignited within her that started her spiritual journey of self-discovery. She had a religious upbringing, but this was the awakening of her personal spirituality that brought her closer to God.

April was now faced with being a single parent and running and managing the house alone. One day she went out to cut the lawn. Have you ever tried to start a lawnmower and when you go to pull the string the first time, nothing happens? Then on the second pull, the lawnmower might make a light noise and you have to continue tugging five, six, seven to ten times before the stubborn thing actually starts? As if that business isn't aggravating enough, when April continued to try to start the lawnmower, she wound up rupturing a vein in her wrist.

When April hurt her wrist, the physical pain she experienced was the straw that broke the camel's back after years of other emotional and physical pain and she realized that it wasn't just her wrist that needed healing – her whole being, body and soul, needed healing. She tried several therapeutic modalities including sound therapy, breath therapy, Body Talk, meditation, Reiki, crystal therapy, and essential oils. She read self-help books, went to conferences, and received professional coaching.

If you have read The Ultimate Guide To Healing Your Past, then you might remember Kelly Meister who tried many different kinds of therapy, some of which helped her and others that didn't. What added to the effect of her therapies was that she learned what she liked doing – working with animals. Like Kelly, April also found what worked best for her – taking time out for herself.

April continued to heal herself and through her memories, she empowered herself and created her own system to help others. Her system has four Rs:

Recognize – the rubble that needs to be cleared before it becomes barriers.

Respond – with a Recovery Plan. This is your blueprint and roadmap. How you respond to your challenges will determine your progress to move forward.

Reevaluate – the Recovery Plan as you rebuild. Make sure it is in alignment with your calling and journey for the future.

Rebalance – the relationships in your life. Make sure those around you enhance your life and it starts with you first. Do you have a healthy and progressive mindset about yourself?

In her book, You Are Not Alone – How To Rise Above Life's Challenges, April takes you on an adventure of inspiration and self-discovery. She describes her four Rs from the standpoint of health, wealth, and spirituality. Some of her other inspirations include things to believe in, it includes belief in yourself, in others, and belief that you are given strength, confidence, and knowledge. She advises the reader to go on a digital diet plan and schedule, and be in your mode.

April said she felt drawn to helping others. While Intel was a job and it paid the bills, helping others was her calling. She does believe that everything that happened to her led to the life she has now. Her advice for everyone is: put yourself on your to-do list and discover the powerful you.

Like April, the story you'll read in the next chapter is about a man who eventually also learned to put himself on his own to do list.

Chapter 9 QR Code

http://www.phenomenalmemory.com/BookResources/video10.htm

Chapter 9

Yes! Please put yourself on your To-Do List!

Nate grew up in a strict Quaker family. Nate remembers going with his mother to take clothes to migrant farm workers and receiving cash from his father that he was expected to give away to worthy causes.

While it is good to help others, Nate developed some beliefs that did not serve him well. One was the belief that you should not do things for yourself, because that was selfish. Another was that he was responsible for everyone else's happiness. The problem was that he never gave anyone a chance to serve him. His focus on taking care of everyone except himself often left him feeling emotionally depleted.

Children can often be our best teachers. Nate and his wife adopted a nine-year-old boy named Darqui. He was a troubled boy with a lot of anger and hurt.

At first, Darqui had no confidence and needed a lot of reassurance. Nate, as the caretaker, was more than happy to give it to him. But one day when Darqui was twelve years old he pushed Nate away. He said, "I hate you for trying to make me happy! Leave me the #%*& alone! I have a right to have my dark side and there was nothing you can do to help me feel better!"

Nate asked him, "Are you sure there is nothing I can do for you?"

"Nothing," Darqui responded. "Worry about your own life!"

Nate reluctantly agreed to give Darqui his space, but this conversation was followed by three months of almost no communication between father and son.

When Darqui started speaking to Nate again Nate just listened and did not try to change his perspective. He realized that it was grandiose of him to think he could change Darqui or anyone else.

Nate then started a path of learning to care for himself. He learned meditation, mindfulness, and to do things for the simple reason that he enjoys them. This includes going to the woods, playing his guitar, and watching sports with friends.

Perhaps the corollary to learning you can't make anyone else happy is when Nate learned you can choose how you feel in any situation. Nate and his wife Anita noticed their daughter, Nikki, was not developing typically. She made poor eye contact with them and seemed uninterested in social interaction. There were signs of autism.

After investigating treatment centers, they decided to seek help from a place in the Berkshire Mountains of Massachusetts called the Option Institute. They work with the child to develop a treatment program and they work with the parents to help them change their beliefs about the child's situation. This is done via a dialogue where they ask questions that help parents question the reasons for their unhappiness.

When Nate had his session with the staff they asked him, "What would happen if you let go of your unhappiness about Nikki's condition?"

Nate responded that if he was not unhappy he might not work hard enough to help Nikki and people might think he was not caring. Then they asked, "Why don't you choose to be happy despite the challenges you face with Nikki?"

This was a liberating moment for Nate. It had never occurred to him that he had a choice to be happy or unhappy. Fortunately, he realized he could choose how he feels in any circumstance.

Nate now knows that he can listen to people and support them, but only they can change themselves. He now counsel's people to take care of themselves and be more self-compassionate. He uses the memories of his Quaker upbringing to help others, but he also learned from his children to take care of himself. It shows the need for balance. Part of balancing your life is to not think of yourself as a victim. The stories in the next chapter are from people who were bullied but still do not see themselves as victims.

Nate Terrell invites you to check out his book, Achieving Self-Compassion: Giving Yourself the Gifts of Happiness and Inner Peace.

Chapter 10 QR Code

http://www.phenomenalmemory.com/BookResources/video11.htm

Chapter 10

You Can Beat The Odds At The Doctor's Office

Modern medicine is starting to accept the mind-body connection, and many doctors accept the idea that we hold energy in our bodies. This includes negative energy, and when we hold too much negative energy in our bodies like anger and fear, illness is likely to develop.

Dr. Manon Bolliger is one such doctor interested in the mind-body connection and its implications and applications in the world of medicine. Trauma, whether it is physical, emotional, spiritual, or psychological has been the focus of her twenty-six years of practice as she had quite a few of her own traumatic experiences, including sexual assault, a challenging relationship, and being diagnosed with Multiple Sclerosis and stage IV cancer.

Stage IV cancer is advanced, and doctors often do not expect the patient to live long after diagnoses. When she was diagnosed, her doctors insisted she have a hysterectomy – but she knew that this was not what was going to save her life. **Rather than succumbing to fear of the odds stacked against her, Dr. Bolliger had a defining moment when she realized that she needed to and could heal herself.**

Dr. Bolliger had become intrigued by the work of an Australian healer named Tom Bowen who in the 1950s had developed a form of physical therapy that involved light touch and gentle manipulation. From her research on Bowen Therapy as well her years in practice as a doctor, she realized that she needed to really listen to her own body in order to heal.

Dr. Bolliger believed at the time of her illness that she was trapped. From her own traumatic experiences, she felt that she was holding on to a negative belief system and negative energy. She learned to let go of the negativity and realized she was actually free and could make a choice. She had another defining and empowering moment when she decided to stop labeling the cancer. She started working with her emotions, listening lovingly to her body, and using the hands-on therapy developed by Tom Bowen. She recovered fully from the cancer without having the hysterectomy.

One of the personal insights Dr. Bolliger discovered was the use that language played in her mental state during her diagnosis. She had kept a journal and she noticed an entry from a year before she discovered the cancer which read, *This is the day my cancer starts*. She believes that she, subconsciously, had triggered the cancer.

Dr. Bolliger has been working with those struggling with trauma using Bowen Therapy for many years. She runs Bowen College in Vancouver, Canada, where the focus is on training Bowen Therapists to connect with their patients through touch and listening. She is the author of *What Patients Don't Say if the Doctor's Don't Ask – The Mindful Patient-Doctor Relationship*, radio host of *Synergy Dialogues in Health*, and Director of Vancouver's Cornerstone Health Centre, which promotes patient consciousness in the healing process.

Dr. Bolliger faced an incredibly frightening cancer diagnoses but was able to empower herself to heal and now she helps other people in similar situations. In the next chapter, you'll read about another young woman who also empowered herself to help others with similar experiences to her own.

Chapter 11 QR Code

http://www.phenomenalmemory.com/BookResources/video12.htm

Chapter 11

La Shawn was a bright young teenager in a Catholic high school. She was a good student and her ambition was to go to law school.

Despite her seemingly bright future, Le Shawn went through a phase where she felt depressed. She had been missing school days due to illness. Around the same time, Le Shawn noticed that one of her friends seemed to be acting differently. Le Shawn thought her friend might be depressed also so she asked her if she was all right and if there was anything she could do to help. Her friend denied that there was anything wrong or that she felt or was acting any differently.

Shortly after this exchange, her friend committed suicide. Le Shawn was devastated. She went through the usual stages people go through when they lose a loved one. She felt angry at her friend for not being more open, sad because she was gone, and she wondered if there was anything she could have done to help and prevent the suicide.

Around the same time, La Shawn was suspended from school. It wasn't quite understood but for some reason, she was not welcome back to the school after her suspension was over. This quick and confusing series of events – her illness, her friend's death, and now being expelled from school – as devastating as they were, empowered La Shawn to make career considerations that were not previously on her agenda.

At seventeen years old, it was time to apply for colleges. La Shawn's lifetime ambition was to major in Political Science and Pre-Law, but when it came time to apply to schools, she had changed her mind. La Shawn now felt that she was called to social work. One of her teachers told her that she had a job lined up when she graduated related to a law degree, and other people told her she was too smart for social work, but La Shawn didn't care. She wanted to be there for any lonely lady, like herself or her friend, who felt suicidal and had no one to talk to and care.

A social worker advocates for their clients. La Shawn wanted to advocate for people whose rights have been violated, particularly members of minority groups, and she wanted to practice in under-served settings.

Today Le Shawn is the lead therapist in a counseling practice she founded called Social Work Diva. It is a counseling service that helps empower women to see their value and strength in times of turmoil and uncertainty. She is married and the proud mother of a toddler. If you want to learn more about La Shawn or her practice, Social Work Diva, you can visit her website at www.socialworkdiva.com.

Similarly to La Shawn, I have memories of being told I should pursue a career other than counseling. People had many different ideas about what kind of career I should aspire to given my gift of a good memory. Many people recommended accounting, but I took one accounting course in high school and was totally bored with it. Since I live near Atlantic City, New Jersey, people wanted to take me into the casinos to count Blackjack cards for them so they could win big money. Many people suggested being a doctor, lawyer, or anything that required a Ph.D.

Given all the suggestions as well as criticisms of the field I had chosen, as I advanced through the counseling profession I always had worries in the back of my mind that I should have chosen a different career.

I was able to shed those doubts though when I learned of the research that the University of California was doing on Hyperthymesia, the technical name for how I can remember so many details of my life. I was excited that now I would be given a chance to use the talent that I have for something practical that could contribute to the world. On the evening of Thursday, October 14, 2010, the researchers at the University contacted me to schedule a date to come in and talk. We settled on Wednesday, February 9, 2011. That night I not only felt excited to participate in the research, but I also felt that a weight was lifted from my shoulders. Now I could stay in my career using my counseling and writing talents and still use my memory to contribute to the world.

Other people with Hyperthymesia are in a variety of careers, including acting, management, human services, and many others. With a master's degree, I actually have more formal education than many of my peers in that group. Consequentially, I no longer feel that I chose the wrong career or should have lived my life differently.

Maybe you are confused about whether or not you chose the right career, or if you are a young adult, whether or not you are on the right career path. If others are telling you that you should do something differently, remember that they do not have all the information about you that is necessary to determine what is truly best for you. There are many things that intelligent people can do in fields that do not have a reputation of being ambitious enough for an intelligent person. It is okay to follow your hunches.

Chapter 12 QR Code

http://www.phenomenalmemory.com/bookresources/video13.htm

Chapter 12

I Refuse To Be The Victim

Gabrielle came from a long lineage of achievers, including many relatives with Ph.D.'s. Perfectionism reigned in her upbringing in other ways, too. Her stepmother subjected her to constant verbal abuse, most of which was accusations that Gabrielle was just too sensitive. She heard this from other family members as well.

In our American culture, high sensitivity is often seen as a handicap. People tell others they are too sensitive as if it was a crippling condition that will prevent them from having any success in this world. Despite Gabrielle's sensitivity, the motto in her family seemed to be that if you make a mistake, you are a total failure.

Perhaps surprisingly, Gabrielle was still a good student and had friends. She was not subject to bullying in school. However, she did exhibit behavior problems. She talked back to the teachers and got involved with drugs. She went through a period where she did not want to think or talk about the future.

Some of these behaviors can be typical of teenagers. Gabrielle shared that she realizes that some of her behavior might have happened with or without her behavior at school. She eventually overcame her apathetic phase and decided to study psychology. She discovered she liked helping others.

After graduation, Gabrielle started a job with a group of psychologists in a small practice. It was a rocky start though as her coworkers seemed to not like her and were acting like they were jealous of her. They went so far as to gossip about her and to tell the head psychologist of the practice that Gabrielle was slandering her on Facebook.

Gabrielle herself started getting some professional therapy and taking medication. Additionally, she involved herself in Buddhist practices which taught her and helped her to release her anger and get to a place where she was able to forgive her coworkers for the difficulty they were putting her through. She still works in the same practice, so in addition to making the right moves to resolve the conflicts at work, she empowered herself internally. Her outlook became: I refuse to be the victim.

Personally, I share Gabrielle's view of refusing to be a victim. I'd like to take you through an exercise to help you better understand what makes a victim, and how sometimes, people choose to be a victim.

Exercise 4 – Recognize The Victim

You may just answer the questions for this exercise without writing them down, but if you would like you can take the time to record them.

Who is the victim in each of the following examples?

- **A young man in high school gets straight As and is an accomplished pianist, but his father is disgusted that he does not play sports.**
- **A boss at work nags and finds fault with everything one of their employees does, but this employee does more work than anyone there. One day the employee walks out because they refuse to take any more abuse.**
- **A person with depression and anxiety goes to therapy and the therapist is warm and caring and teaches them good coping skills. The client decides that they have no connection with the therapist and goes elsewhere.**
- **A lady who has not had much luck with men finds a man who is attractive, has a good job and does**

everything for her. She leaves him and a month later is back with her abusive ex.

If you think the way most people do, the last example is obvious. The lady who left her good boyfriend has low self-esteem and was like a cleaned pig returning to their mud puddle. The good boyfriend may have been upset at losing her, but he felt the loving feelings which made him the happy one. He is more likely to find a woman who appreciates him in the future.

The father in the first example makes himself the victim. He has reasons to be happy and proud of his son but he chooses to be angry and disappointed in him for something he does not do.

In the second example, the boss is the victim for the same reason. The boss has reasons to be happy about their good employee but instead, they focus on the negative. The employee chose not to be a victim by leaving. Sure you could say that the employee is the victim because they are now unemployed while the boss still has his job, but the boss probably does not appreciate anyone and the former employee will work hard to find another job.

The client who decided they have no connection with their therapist even though the therapist was warm and caring and taught them healthy ways to cope has made themselves a victim. Maybe subconsciously they don't want to get better and are just looking for someone to entertain them. Consequentially, the client is the victim because they are not truly seeking out the help they need in order to grow.

Essentially, a victim is someone who chooses to be unhappy despite there being many reasons for them to be happy. Gabrielle chose to not view herself as defective and she chose not to be unhappy because of her sensitivity, nor does she view herself as the one who gets abused more than others. She has empowered herself by embracing her past and has used her experiences to be a more effective counselor to people who

have been through the same things she has been through. Her future career ambitions include working with clients who are intellectually gifted but sensitive, as well as counseling bullied children.

Speaking of bullying advocates, if you read the first book in this series, *Heal Your Memories, Change Your Life*, you may recall Kate. Kate was bullied in every imaginable way from seventh through twelfth grade. There were rumors that she slept with the English teacher and the whole football team. Kids walked by her while she minded her own business on the computer and called her a whore. They also made fake MySpace pages of whores and sent them to her. They made special efforts to cyber bully her even on Christmas, her birthday, and when she was on a family vacation at Disney World.

One night, a girl from school who was a former friend of Kate's assaulted Kate on the street. Kate wound up hitting the girl out of self-defense, but afterward, Kate's mother, who didn't completely understand the situation, drove Kate to the girl's house so Kate could apologize.

I asked Kate what empowered her through those dark troubled times. She shared that she always had a sense that her life would improve. She believed that there is a purpose to her life and she would not give up because she needed to live that purpose. The flame of hope was never completely extinguished.

College was better for Kate. She had good grades, was president of her junior class and school representative of the National Collegiate Honor Society in her senior year.

Kate's belief that her life would get better and purposeful was quite prophetic. After college, she joined the National Speakers Bureau. She was not afraid to tell her story of how she was bullied. She now goes all over the country and tells her story at conferences and schools. She has been featured on nationally syndicated and international radio shows.

There is a saying that the best way to get back at your tormentors is to live happily now. Today, Kate is happily married to her husband, CJ. They got married in a beautiful cathedral church and had their wedding reception in a baseball stadium. They live on a farm in New Jersey, vacation frequently, and have a large supportive circle of family and friends. She used her memories of being bullied to empower herself to help others and to also remember to be good to herself.

Chapter 13 QR Code

http://www.phenomenalmemory.com/bookresources/video14.htm

Chapter 13

What Empowerment is...and What it is not

You have now read some incredible stories about how people faced strong opposition and thrived despite that opposition. Claudio could have easily given up his dream of a career in baseball and instead be working in a career he doesn't like. Kelley and Sande could have become bitter fearful people who do not trust anyone. Dr. Bolliger could have let herself succumb to the cancer. Gabrielle and Kate could have become cynical or shut themselves off from the mean, bullying world. Similarly, Steve could have hated his father and done nothing to help anyone else with PTSD. David could have spent his life as a homeless person. Daisy could have ignored the spiritual experiences that shaped her life. Amy could have let herself be scared and not used her talents to help others. Alceen could have seen herself as a lifetime victim, April could have spent her life being bitter about the loss of her husband, and Nate could still be a self-sacrificing martyr.

The life choices that these people made all show that you can overcome anything and empower yourself by turning it into a positive. If there is one common thread that they all had it was that they believed they could change, they knew what kind of person they wanted to become, and they took action to become that person.

While these stories exemplify true and meaningful empowerment, some people think that they are empowering themselves but unfortunately, they have the wrong idea of what empowerment is. Picture the short boy who has been picked on all through grade school and middle school because of his height. Once he gets to high school, he decides that he will act tough and not take any bullying or disrespect from anyone. Then he becomes the kid who yells and curses at everyone, and now he's not only the short kid but also the obnoxious kid that no one likes.

Many teenage gang members who later become criminals were abused at home. Their false sense of empowerment as the person with the gun that you better not look at the wrong way comes from taking out the aggression they have built up, from being abused, on society as a whole. They are angry at their abuser or abusers and everyone they encounter pays.

If you remember my four-step technique for empowering yourself from chapter one, you can see how the people whom I interviewed unwittingly applied it and the people in the hypothetical examples that I just gave did not apply it. For the angry teenager and the gang member, they haven't changed their beliefs. They maintain their belief that the world and the people in it are bad and that they are not well liked. Then they make themselves more hateful. They do not imagine and think of themselves as the person they could be, they do not feel the feelings associated with the person they could be, and they take the wrong actions.

Anger may be the most deceptive emotion that we experience. A person makes themselves angry to deny that they are feeling hurt, afraid, sad, or any other feeling that their pride denies them. Many boys and men believe that it is okay to get angry but not okay to feel scared or sad. You do not encounter many men who will walk up to another man and say, "You hurt my feelings," or, "I am scared of you." They are more likely to yell or pick a fight. While this behavior is more often seen coming from men, women can make this mistake, too.

When someone expresses anger, they think they are powerful and in control. Ironically, the people around them see that they are out of control and can feel intimidated because they aren't sure how out of control the person will get. If you ever knew anyone who never seemed to express anger it is likely that they know that to vent their anger is to lose control, and they would rather stay in control of themselves and empower themselves.

Exercise 5 – Own Your Memories, Don't Let Them Own You

You will need a pen and paper for this exercise, or a Word document.

Look at the following situations and decide whether the person empowered themselves or not.

- **A young man in high school decides that he is tired of not fitting in with the cliques. He decides to change the way he dresses, his mannerisms and reaches out to his peers again.**
- **A father brings his three sons and youngest daughter who is only ten to a gym to learn wrestling. The boys have a moderate interest but his daughter falls in love with it and decides this is a sport for her to pursue.**
- **A young man who has a degree in psychology looks for a job for a half a year. He does not get one so he decides that helping people is not as important as job security. He then becomes a pen pusher at his township office because he thinks it is more realistic and he knows he'll one day get a pension.**
- **A visiting nurse who is dealing with an obnoxious and disrespectful patient in his home. He even told her that a particular female corpse looked better than her. She quits nursing and vows to work in a munitions factory to exterminate humanity.**
- **A young man in college who decides that he is not that smart and not good at managing his money so**

he decides to enter a religious order where everything will be paid for.

- Another young man who is highly intelligent and could be successful in any career he chooses but gets stuck on the idea that "kids today" need to be straightened out and takes a job as a teacher after college because he thinks he's the one to do it. He frequently verbally abuses his students in an attempt to discipline them. He gets married and has kids but abuses them, too.

- A young lady who was a victim of incest becomes promiscuous and feels proud that she is not afraid of sex.

- A retired schoolteacher, who after spending her life up to that point helping other people, decides to take a new job in her local horticultural display center giving guided tours. She doesn't need the money or the benefits, she just does it because it's fun.

- An elderly widow who decides that she is tired of the world and life without her husband will not be any fun. The widow maintains her religious belief that suicide is not the answer, so she isolates herself from her friends and does not even let them in when they come knocking on her door to visit. She never leaves the house except to go grocery shopping and to church.

- A man who used to fly planes, play sports, and be active is now limited after a heart attack. He decides that it doesn't matter if painting and crocheting aren't seen by the world as masculine hobbies, he's going to give them a try anyway and finds he enjoys them.

So we have some examples of how different people coped with seemingly unhappy situations. Before moving ahead, write down who you think is empowered and who isn't, and why before moving on.

Now that you have completed this exercise, we are going to take each situation and examine what would and would not have been the empowered way to handle it.

In the first situation, the young man decided to change. In order to mimic the mannerisms and behaviors of the popular kids, he had to observe them. Then he had to change his beliefs about what is possible for himself. Instead of believing that he is not a likable person, he decided he could be popular if he just changed a few things. Then he had to picture himself as a popular kid and feel the feelings. If he had skipped this step, the changes in his behavior would have seemed unnatural and fake. He needed to do these steps before he took action.

Some of you might have thought this was not empowering because he was not being himself. Have you ever been frustrated with something and expressed that you wanted to make a change but someone told you, "No, be yourself. You can't be like those other people because you are you."? I have memories of being told that and memories of these remarks making me angrier and more frustrated than I was to begin with.

While Dr. Seuss said, "Today you are You, that is truer than true. There is no one alive who is Youer than You," I think part of being you includes whether you like or dislike the results you are creating in your life. There are plenty of people, myself included, who are naturally introverted but have learned to act as an extrovert because they did not want to be deprived of enjoying social contact. So if anyone tells you that you can't do something because you don't have the talent or the personality, remember that you can empower yourself to do it.

Sometimes your desires could go against the image of you that other people maintain, like the second example of a ten-year-old girl who likes wrestling. It's not typical for girls to like wrestling, but this particular girl can and will empower herself if she pursues her passion and does not concern herself with what people think. **If she unwillingly yielded to social pressures and did whatever the people around her wanted her to do to fit the social norm, she would yield her power to them.**

Many young adults have a sense of idealism in their younger days as they try to find their way in the world. Some of them stay that way but many yield to the pressures of what the world thinks they are supposed to be or do. The young man who fails to obtain employment in counseling and decides to take a local municipal job is disempowering himself as he is allowing the world to tell him that job security and a cozy pension are more important than obtaining a career doing something that he enjoys. If he really felt convicted that counseling was the way for him to go, he could volunteer in a psychiatric hospital or take the township job temporarily while earning a master's degree in counseling or social work to expand his job prospects.

All of these examples are hypothetical and to the best of my knowledge fictional. The example of the nurse who quit caring for the obnoxious patient was actually a character from a scene in the play and the movie, *The Man Who Came To Dinner*. In this play, a man gets injured when visiting some people and while he receives treatment at the hospital, he is totally obnoxious to those trying to help him. He verbally abuses the nurse as in the example above and he abuses the family but they can't get rid of him because he keeps injuring himself. The nurse gets to where she has finally had enough abuse and says she always wanted to help people but after dealing with this particular man, she has decided to leave nursing and work in a munitions factory to exterminate humanity.

This is an excellent example of how not to empower yourself. Any memory that you respond to by becoming hateful and wanting to hurt people, animals, or anything in the world is not empowering. People who have had memories of abuse always have a choice whether they will empower themselves by becoming strong and compassionate or disempower themselves by seeking revenge on the world or a segment of it.

Having worked in the mental health field for twenty-eight years, basically half my life, I know there are days when it seems that I was not helping anyone or days where I was taking abuse from people whom I was trying to help. Other times it just seemed that no one was motivated to help themselves. However, those days are few and far between compared to the days when it is a joy to help others. I use my memory to recall good times when I was able to help clients and they appreciated it.

I also enjoyed college teaching when I did it. There was an exercise we used to do in class where I traced the time lines of Mother Theresa's life and Saddam Hussein's life. I wanted to show the class how we are all motivated by moving away from pain and moving towards pleasure. For Mother Theresa, pleasure meant helping people even in the most deplorable conditions. Pain to her meant witnessing suffering. For Saddam Hussein, pleasure meant having power over others and killing anyone who got in his way. Pain meant losing his power.

If you use your memories of experiencing pain and hurt in a way that you want to help others and yourself then you are empowered. However, if you use it in a way that you want others to suffer as much as you did, you are definitely not empowered.

Many people feel this way when someone else really hurt them. For example, if a man lost his wife to another man, he might have fantasies of hurting the man who stole his wife. However, that will not empower him – it will frustrate him. If he does not get

92

revenge he will continue to seethe while the other man is having the time of his life with his new girlfriend. If he decides to actually hurt the man who stole his wife, he will probably wind up in jail which is definitely not an empowering place to be.

Any decision that you make that is based on your weaknesses without including strengths will not be empowering. In the next example, the young man who decides to enter a religious order because he thinks he isn't smart enough for anything else and can't manage his money will not find satisfaction in a religious order unless he has a calling for it.

So how can someone like that empower himself? He could try different things to see if he does have the smarts and skills necessary, or he could find something he likes doing and practice it until he gets better at it. He could also learn the basics of money management either through a course or a self-help book. If it turns out that he has an addiction to spending money, he can go to therapy.

Then there is the man who is intelligent with many career opportunities in front of him but seethes with anger about "kids today." He decides it is his job to straighten out the youth. He gets a job in a school and is the mean teacher that nobody wants to have. He abuses his own children then loses everything, including his teaching certificate when a neighbor calls Child Protective Services and he earns himself a record.

This man could have empowered himself by choosing a career where he had no contact with children and where he could enjoy himself, rather than choosing a profession that puts him right in the middle of the thing that frustrates him the most. He also could have empowered himself by going to therapy for anger management so that he could control himself around his own children.

My brother, who is the family class clown, posts on Facebook about "kids today." He often makes fun of the travesties of life. For example, recently he posted, "Kids today with their cyberbullying. When we were kids, if you didn't like another kid, you would sneak up behind him with tape and a 'Kick Me' sign, stuck the sign to his back and ran away." **You should all know from other things I've written that I do not condone bullying, but humor can be a way to empower yourself and the man in the example above could empower himself by learning to laugh at the differences in the generations.**

For the example of the young lady who was a victim of incest and then turned promiscuous, this is not empowerment. It is foolish risk taking. She could empower herself by going to therapy and working through what happened to her. She could also learn what it means to have real and positive relationships with men.

Empowerment is for all ages. A retired school teacher who dedicated her life to helping her students and raising her family now wants to enjoy her retirement, so she takes a job in her local horticultural display center because she simply would enjoy the job. It could be anywhere: the local zoo, a thrift store, political headquarters. It all depends on what she would like doing.

My aunt Sheila spent her career teaching in the school systems in Camden, New Jersey. She retired at fifty-five and took the job of a tour guide at Longwood Gardens in Kennett Square, Pennsylvania, one of the largest horticultural display centers in the world. She did that for more than fifteen years.

Many people do not empower themselves after retirement. They stop doing things and just sit at home bored and twiddling their thumbs. It can be okay to sit at home if you are content with that. Some retirees travel or get involved with the grandchildren. **As long as you do what you like and feel fulfilled doing it, you are empowering yourself.**

Conversely, the woman who isolates herself after her husband's death is not empowering herself. She is just giving up on life and not appreciating what she still has. She could choose to empower herself by continuing with her friends and involving herself in the life she still has.

Finally, the man who can't be physically active anymore and decides to take up new sedentary hobbies is definitely empowered. He is reinventing himself, finding things to do that make him happy, and not worrying whether what he does is masculine enough or whether anyone approves.

As you can see there are many right and wrong ways to empower yourself through your memories. In the next chapter, I will show you how to empower yourself through memories of not having enough.

Chapter 14 QR Code

http://www.phenomenalmemory.com/bookresources/video15.htm

Chapter 14

Give yourself those things you did not Receive in Childhood

Some people spend their whole adult life trying to get what they felt they had too little of as a child or teenager. You can empower yourself to meet your needs now if those needs were not met in the past. Here are some examples.

Example 2 – Making Up For The Past

- Someone who grew up in a completely dull and boring home with bare white walls, no luxuries, and of course no vacations. This person looks back and thinks that they have no memories of being exposed to learning and life experiences, and the memory includes resentment of their parents for this. Conversely, as an adult, they have a good home with great furniture and décor, they go to interesting places for vacation and expose their children to all that life has to offer.
- Someone who had no religious or spiritual experiences during childhood now goes to church every week and to Bible studies during the week.
- Someone who experienced no love and affection growing up now highly emphasizes love and caring in their own family.
- Growing up consisted of constantly going to community events and being forced to be sociable. Now as an adult, they value their quiet time and have just a couple of close friends.

With these examples, you can see that you can choose how you want to empower yourself through your memories. If you have good memories from certain areas of your life, you can choose to continue with similar activities as an adult. For example, if you were exposed to the arts and mom and dad even bought you a one thousand dollar painting for your college dorm room, you can continue to appreciate the arts even after you are settled in your own life and home. If you grew up having good experiences at church, you can continue to have the church be important in your life. If you grew up in a loving and affectionate household, you can also raise your own family that way.

On the opposite end of the spectrum, and similar to the examples above, if you had bad experiences of having too little growing up, you can choose to empower yourself to meet your needs now.

No Fun Nancy who grew up in a boring home and lacked meaningful experiences as a child chose to empower herself as an adult to have a more adventurous and entertaining life to make up for her boring upbringing.

Religionless Ralph who felt deprived after being denied any spiritual experiences growing up chose to empower himself to seek out a church he could grow in and experience God for himself.

Lonely Laura who didn't get the hugs and kisses she needed growing up chose to empower herself to display affection with her own children while raising them, making sure they were showered with all the love they could ever hope for.

Social Sally who was forced to go to community events chose to empower herself to prioritize quiet time in her daily life to maintain her sanity. She also chose a lifestyle in which she only needs a few close friends to fulfill her social needs.

There is one trap of empowering yourself through your memories of deprivation. It is possible to become too obsessed with doing the activity you did not do as a child. Suppose that dull and boring home life caused you to become a hedonist. You now indulge in too many earthly pleasures, such as drinking too much or entertaining other destructive addictions. You feel that you need your senses stimulated all of the time or you will get depressed. This is not empowerment, and therapy may be necessary.

Throughout this book, we have referenced dramatic memories that people used to empower themselves. In the next chapter, you will learn to empower yourself even if your memories were more ordinary.

Chapter 15 QR Code

http://www.phenomenalmemory.com/bookresources/video16.htm

Chapter 15

What if my Memories are not that Interesting or Dramatic?

As you went through this book and read the stories, you may have thought that your life has been plain and pedestrian compared to the people that you read about. You may think, *I was never homeless on the street, My stomach never burst,* or *I was never sexually abused.* Or you might think, *I was teased a little in school but not beat up,* or *I had a tough boss once but I was never stabbed in the back* (figuratively of course).

We can all use memories to empower ourselves. Maybe you failed to make the sports team or the band in school. Maybe your younger sibling was praised for everything and you were laughed at when you attempted anything. Maybe your sister got straight As and was a gifted ballerina, but when you decided to be your own person and try out for the football team, your parents' reaction was, okay if you really want to get hurt. Here are some more examples of ordinary experiences turned empowering experiences.

Example 3 – Everyday Memories Can Be Empowering

- **As a child, the other kids around you took advantage of how nice you were by stealing your toys and incidentally the toys always wound up broken. You now teach personal empowerment seminars and encourage others to stand up for themselves.**

- **When you are around other people, you are the quiet one. You now write novels and paint because you always observed a lot in your quietness.**

- You were the one who always played with children younger than you, and now you are a child psychologist.
- Your family never went on vacation. Now you are a travel agent and go on a paid vacation five times a year.
- You grew up poor, but now you are very successful in business and a master of financial management.
- Mom and dad were busy working and you had to take care of your younger siblings. This taught you responsibility and now you are successful at work but have learned to be silly and childlike when the situation allows. You might even be the one and only adult who gets on rollerblades or kayaks with the children in the neighborhood.
- You did not have friends as a child or as a teenager but now you entertain guests in your home frequently and you go to parties every week. You always enjoy these occasions and you never tire of being around people.
- You were a bully as a child but now you make anti-bullying speeches at school because you learned how much bullying hurts. You do this because you want to and not out of guilt.
- You were a very bossy and mean child, teenager, and adult. Then you became a doctor and realized that everyone has feelings and, come to think of it, people are alike in many ways and you have become as compassionate as you used to be callous.
- Your spouse died at a young age. After a year or two of bitterness, you now find joy and satisfaction counseling other bereaved people.

What do you see that is uniform through these examples? Think for a minute.

In every one of these examples, as ordinary or mundane as they seem, the person was given an opportunity to make a change. If we go back through the list, there are opposite actions the person could have chosen that would have had profound implications on their lives.

Sweetness Seminar Leader could have remained the person that everyone takes advantage of. She also could have allowed herself to progress into a bitter and angry person.

Joe Quiet could have lost interest in life and become a recluse.

Peter Pan could have been an immature adult after spending all that time with children younger than he was instead of using his talent for good.

Vacationless Vera could have stayed that way and had a boring adult life.

Poor Robbed Paul could have turned to drugs and street fighting instead of the business world.

Patty The Parent Child could have become a bitter and mean adult after spending her childhood taking care of other kids instead of playing and having fun.

Antisocial Annie could have become a recluse just like Joe Quiet.

Brian Bully could have been a bullying adult and a doctor who did not listen well to his patients.

Bonnie Bereaved could have spent the rest of her life angry with the world and with God for taking her husband so early in life.

All of these fictional people could have made their adult lives more dramatic and disempowering than their childhoods were by ignoring their everyday, ordinary memories. They didn't see their memories as mundane though and they used them to make good choices, as did the real people I interviewed for the stories that you read. They all took their memories and empowered themselves rather than seeing those memories as an excuse to make bad choices.

I imagine that since you purchased this book and have progressed this far into it that you have at least one memory that you feel holds you back and does not empower you. Previously we did an exercise with your dramatic memories. In the next exercise, you will pick a memory that was not dramatic and think of how you can empower yourself through it.

Exercise 6 – Empower Yourself Through Ordinary Memories

You will need a pen and paper, or a Word document.

1. **Pick a memory that often surfaces in your mind. Pick something that if you were an outsider who does not know you, you would think that what happened was not a big deal.**
2. **Write a description of the memory. Use as much detail as you can. What does everything look like? Who was there? What sounds did you hear? What sensations did you feel? How do you feel recalling this memory?**
3. **Write any beliefs that you developed from the memory. For example, what does it say about you, other people, and the world?**
4. **Ask yourself, what is a bad way that this memory could affect you? For example, suppose you stole something as a child. You were caught but the juvenile courts decided to just have your parents pay a small fine and you had to write an essay about why crime is not the way. If there was no real punishment, then a bad way this memory could affect you is that you might now think**

crime is okay and even if you get caught, nothing serious will happen.

5. Now ask yourself what a good way to respond to this experience would be. From the previous example, you could decide that crime does not pay and then decide to become a police officer.

6. Review both the bad ways and the good ways that this memory could affect you, and using this information, write how you can now empower yourself through that memory.

Now that you have completed this exercise, you can go and live your empowered life. Remember that you can apply what you learned to any situation in your life. You can do this exercise for any memories that surface, whether the memory deserves an Oscar Award or not.

In my counseling practice, I often have clients who say that their life looks good on the outside. Maybe they have a good spouse, great children, and a good job. Their families do not understand why they are depressed or anxious and need to go to therapy. Often as the therapy progresses we uncover a memory that causes them to feel this way. No matter what the memory is if you need to heal it, do it. You are not weak or dysfunctional if people do not understand why something would bother you.

In the next chapter, you will learn how to empower yourself now even if your circumstances now are not as good as your memories of the past. You can always find a way.

Chapter 16 QR Code

http://www.phenomenalmemory.com/bookresources/video17.htm

Chapter 16

Those were the Days I Felt Empowered

What if you know what empowerment feels like, and you've experienced it in your youth or even a few years ago, but now your circumstances aren't what they used to be? Certainly, no one would question an elderly person who feels that they are not as smart or as physically capable as they used to be. However, even young people can feel that they do not do as well as they used to. You can empower yourself through at any age and in any circumstance. Let me show you some examples and then we'll discuss them.

Example 4 – Those Were The Days

- **A man who used to be physically active with a landscaping career and athletic abilities was in a car accident and now needs a wheelchair to get around.**
- **A young man with a promising career who has put on weight since high school and now as a twenty-two-year old says that he got more dates in high school than he does now.**
- **A young lady whose grades slipped because she took on too much in the most recent semester in college now feels that she can't do anything anymore and does not want to think about the future because she does not believe she has good options. The bad semester will go on her permanent record.**
- **A fifty-year-old man who loses his job because of outsourcing and does not want to move to Bangalore, India, where his work has gone. He needs to finish**

putting his three offspring through college but can't stomach starting from the bottom of the corporate ladder again.

- An aspiring actress who suddenly feels that she has no hope in the industry because a reporter and photographer decided she had the ugliest dress at a big Gala.
- A woman of faith who attended the same congregation for ten years and was heavily involved in several ministries for the congregation was voted out of her position in those ministries for political reasons.
- A college professor who worked hard and gave his all during his whole career for his dream of being the department chair but when the position opened up, another younger professor was chosen for political reasons.
- A college athlete whose aspirations were to make the sport she plays her career but was injured and can't play anymore.
- A high school girl whose life seemed to end on the day before the prom when her boyfriend broke up with her.
- A college graduate who was always a top student and voted "Most Likely to Succeed" but still works at their job in a restaurant three years after graduation because the economy is down.

If you were paying attention to anything I've said up to now, then you may have surmised that all of these people still have plenty of opportunities to continue empowering themselves to a better future.

Willie Wheelchair could swallow his pride and compete in wheelchair racing. He could also take on more sedentary hobbies and maybe discover he has talents he didn't know he had.

Big Bob could empower himself to regain his self-confidence with women. He could also see his situation as an opportunity to start eating better and maybe exercise when he has time.

Bella Bad Semester could reexamine her priorities to determine if having perfect grades is really the most important thing in life. She can also use this experience to learn not to be so hard on herself. She could even go so far as to empower herself to be nice to herself sometimes, maybe by meditating and eating right. At the very least, she could use this experience to remember no

Joe Jobless At Midlife can share his experience with his young adult children and the whole family could empower themselves towards a better financial future with more shared responsibility.

Fashion Senseless Denise who was bullied by the media about her dress could visit a consultant and try out for new roles as she sees this episode as a temporary setback.

Bunny Blackballed could spend some time thinking about all the good that she did for the church she attended and empower herself to continue serving even if it's not within an organized ministry. She could also try to find a church with a more Christian attitude and see it as an opportunity to strengthen her faith in God.

Paul Professor can immerse himself more in his teaching and find additional things in his life to feel good about. He could also empower himself to pursue a department chair position at another college.

Josephine Jock could consider a career path like Claudio from chapter three and still be engaged in the sport she loves from the sidelines.

There is a better man for Not The Prom Queen Pauline and she now has a nice dress to save for him. She can use this experience to empower herself to continue dating and not settle for anyone who treats her with less respect and honor than what she deserves.

Finally, George Graduate still has a job despite the bad economy and when he finds a job becoming of his education, he will appreciate it that much more.

As these examples show, whether you are sixteen, fifty, or eighty-five, and even it if seems like your best days are behind you, you can still make these the days to empower yourself.

Chapter 17 QR Code

http://www.phenomenalmemory.com/bookresources/video18.htm

Chapter 17

Put it all Together for a Wonderful Present and Future

If you have read all three of my books, you now know how to heal yourself from the effects of traumatic and hurtful memories, how to learn from your memories, and how to empower yourself from your memories.

Heal Your Memories, Change Your Life taught you that you can release the unwanted feelings from past experiences. That book had many exercises in it that I use in my counseling practice to help others release the pain from hurtful or traumatic memories of their past. You learned that even if you can't let go of the memory itself, you can still release the negative and painful emotions associated with that memory.

The Ultimate Guide To Healing Your Past taught you that you have a treasure trove of learnings embedded in all of your memories. I showed you exercises you could do to learn important lessons from any memories that you want to, good or bad, to better your life. I also shared stories of some amazing people who used horrific past experiences like war and abuse to learn valuable lessons and direct their lives where they wanted them to go.

Now, *Empowering Yourself Through Your Memories* has taught you that you can empower yourself through your memories. You've heard some more amazing stories of people who used their memories and experiences to empower themselves and reach their goals regardless of what stood in their way. Hopefully, you've done the exercises as you read and can see that you also can empower yourself and heal from any bad memories and reach your goals!

If you would like to continue learning more ways to heal your memories or empower yourself to change your life, you can go to my website, www.phenomenalmemory.com. If you haven't had a chance to read my other books but would like to, you can find them on my web page. You can also find more information on my Facebook page, Phenomenal Memory, and on my Facebook fan page. If you need additional professional coaching to heal your memories and to change your life, I am also available by email at frank@phenomenalmemory.com.

Afterword

I hope you have enjoyed reading *Empower Yourself Through Your Memories* and have learned how to empower yourself. Whether you used the examples of the people who were interviewed, benefitted from the exercises, or increased your confidence, you have been on an exciting journey of personal empowerment. This is a journey that you can take for the rest of your life. With each passing day, you can learn from every experience and every memory that surfaces. Here are the links to my other books:

Heal Your Memories, Change Your Life
http://www.phenomenalmemory.com/books/healmemories.htm

Memory Brain Exercises
http://www.phenomenalmemory.com/books/brainexcercises.htm

The Ultimate Guide to Healing Your Past
http://www.phenomenalmemory.com/books/healmemories2.htm

Contributors

I would like to express my deepest thanks to the following people for their assistance and for allowing me to share their stories.

***

Claudio Reilsono for showing everyone that you can hold on to a dream when you persevere even in the face of naysayers. I look forward to working with you on some future projects.

***

Steve Sparks for being a great example of how you can forgive the past, including family members. You have also showed that you can start the process of forgiving and letting go at any age. Here is Steve's information:

Steve's charity, Kickstarter Projects:
https://www.kickstarter.com/projects/757199121/i-worry-about-the-kids

Steve's Author page on Amazon:
http://www.amazon.com/Steve-Sparks/e/B0070CJDCM/ref=ntt_dp_epwbk_0

Steve's popular blog at www.survivethriveptsd.com He has over 800 blog posts published so you'll want to use the archives and search feature on his blog.

Steve's Facebook Pages:
https://www.facebook.com/stephen.h.sparks/?ref=bookmarks
https://www.facebook.com/profile.php?id=1848131331

Steve's LinkedIn Account:
https://www.linkedin.com/?trk=nav_logo

***

Daisy Seferoglou and **Amy Oestrecher** for demonstrating by example how you can overcome any physical malady and become successful.

Amy Oestecher's Links

Speaking: https://www.amyoes.com/hire-me/motivational-speaking/

Gutless & Grateful: The Deliciously Inspiring One-Woman Musical Comedy Show Page: https://www.amyoes.com/gutless
To book her show: amyoes.com/imprints

Patreon page (to donate): patreon.com/amyo

Free eBooks on art: amyoes.com/create

Speaking tips: amyoes.com/discover

Amy's speaking information, including videos, references, topics and media: https://www.amyoes.com/press-kit/

Amy's *Huffington Post* column: huffingtonpost.com/amy-oestreicher

Amy's writing portfolio: https://www.amyoes.com/writing-portfolio/

Learn about Amy's *#LoveMyDetour* Movement: https://amyoes.com/2015/12/08/are-you-a-detourist-watch-this-video-to-find-out/

What's a Detourist? https://www.amyoes.com/whats-a-detourist/

See Amy's weekly guest feature where she has a fellow Detourist write about a detour in their life: https://www.amyoes.com/category/why-not-wednesday/

Amy's upcoming book, *My Beautiful Detour*: https://www.amyoes.com/book

Amy's writing for *The Mighty*: http://themighty.com/author/amy-oestreicher/

Amy's Mixed Media Art: https://www.amyoes.com/galleries

***

David Everett for your inspiring story of courage and survival and how you came out the other end.

***

Kelley Kitley and **Sandra Chen** for having the courage to share their stories of past abuse and having the courage to overcome it, help others, and develop into the people they are with all their successes.

Kelley Kitley, Serendipitous Psychotherapy, LLC, is the author of the book, *My Self*, her autobiography about survival. To learn more about Kelley, please visit her website at www.kelleykitley.com.

***

Sandra Chen's Links

Book, *Serious Games: Games That Educate, Train, and Inform*:
https://www.amazon.com/Serious-Games-Educate-Train-Inform/dp/1592006221/ref=sr_1_1?s=books&ie=UTF8&qid=1476705928&sr=1-1&keywords=%22Sande+Chen%22

***

Alceen Ford Megget and **April Joy Ford** for overcoming combinations of abuse and loss and using it to inspire others.

April Ford's Links

Website: www.joysofyah.com

Radio Show: www.voiceamerica.com/show/2458/you-are-not-alone

Free *You Are Not Alone* eBook: www.myjoyagain.com

***

Nate Terrell for being my friend and living the healthy idea of being good to yourself. For more information about self-compassion, please visit the following links.

Website: www.achievingselfcompassion.com

Nate invites you to check out his book, *Achieving Self-Compassion: Giving Yourself the Gifts of Happiness and Inner Peace.*

***

Dr. Manon Bolliger, ND, for being an incredible example of healing yourself from an, allegedly, incurable disease and dedicating your life to the health of others. More information about Dr. Bolliger can be found at the following links:

Website: www.drmanon.com

Bowen College: www.bowencollege.com

Cornerstone Health Centre: www.cornerstonehealthcentre.ca

Telephone: 604 732 6222

***

La Shawn Paul, you are an inspiration to everyone who is stuck in their choices of career and to everyone who needs to overcome the effects of unfair treatment.

Website: www.socialWorkDiva.com

Instagram: @SocialWorkDiva

Facebook: www.facebook.com/thesocialworkdiva

***

Gabrielle Loher and **Kate Ecke** for inspiring people all over the world wo need to overcome the effects of bullying.

Gabrielle's Links

Website: http://www.GabrielleLoehr.com

Twitter: https://twitter.com/Gabriellewins

Google: https://plus.google.com/+GabrielleLoehr

LinkedIn: https://www.linkedin.com/in/gabrielleloehr

Mindful Living podcast: http://mindfullivingpodcast.libsyn.com/

Kate's Link

Website: KateMacHugh.com

***

Jim Melonic for the wonderful cover picture.

***

Nina Spearman, as always, for your professional editing.

***

Dr. Richard Blonna for your introduction and your past coaching when I first started writing

About the Author

Frank Healy is a Licensed Professional Counselor and Certified Life Coach in the State of New Jersey. He is classified with Hyperthymesia or Highly Superior Autobiographical Memory (HSAM) by the University of California. Frank remembers events from every day of his life for the past 49. This includes the day of the week, the weather, news, and personal events. Frank lives with his wife, Janet, in Dennisville, New Jersey, and works as a therapist at AtlantiCare Behavioral Health and Associates for Life Enhancement. Frank's other books include:

Heal Your Memories, Change Your Life
http://www.phenomenalmemory.com/books/healmemories.htm

Memory Brain Exercises
http://www.phenomenalmemory.com/books/brainexcercises.htm

The Ultimate Guide to Healing Your Past
http://www.phenomenalmemory.com/books/healmemories2.htm

Frank has been a guest on the *Michael Smerconish Radio Show*. He has been a guest on *True Life Academy* and *Be the Star You Are* with Cynthia Brian. He has been on the CBS and *NBC New Health Check*. You can contact Frank at his website www.phenomenalmemory.com or email him at frank@phenomenalmemory.com

Resources

American Psychiatric Association (2013). *Diagnostic and Statistical Manual of Mental Disorders*, 5th Edition: DSM-5. American Psychiatric Publishing.

Bollinger, Dr. Manon. (February 26, 2016). Personal interview.

Chen, Sande. (February 28, 2016). Personal interview.

Dr. Seuss. *Goodreads* (Website). Retrieved from https://www.goodreads.com/author/quotes/61105.Dr_Seuss Accessed on May 3, 2017.

Ecke, Kate Machugh. (February 23, 2016). Personal interview.

Everett, David. (March 4, 2016). Personal interview.

Ford-Meggett, Alceen. (March 1, 2016). Personal interview.

Ford, April Joy. (April 1, 2016). Personal interview.

"Keeping Up with the Kardashians." *Wikipedia* (Website). Retrieved from https://en.wikipedia.org/wiki/Keeping_Up_with_the_Kardashians. Accessed on May 3, 2017.Kitley, Kelley. (February 24, 2016). Personal interview.

"LeBron James." *Wikipedia* (Website). Retrieved from https://en.wikipedia.org/wiki/LeBron_James. Accessed on May 3, 2017.

Loeher, Gabrielle. (February 29,2016). Personal interview.

Oestecher, Amy. (March 6, 2016). Personal interview.

Paul, Le Shawn. (April 10, 2016). Personal interview.

Resilino, Claudio. (February 26, 2016). Personal interview.

Seferglou, Daisy. (February 28, 2016). Personal interview.

Sparks, Steve. (February 26, 2016). Personal interview.

Terrell, Nate. (March 8, 2016). Personal interview.

Wallis, Hal B. (Executive Producer) & Keighley, William (Director). (1942). The Man who came to Dinner [Motion Picture]. USA:Warner Brothers.

www.ingramcontent.com/pod-product-compliance
Lightning Source LLC
Chambersburg PA
CBHW071157280526
45787CB00002B/531